Essential Learning Theories

Essential Learning Theories

Applications to Authentic Teaching Situations

Andrew P. Johnson

ROWMAN & LITTLEFIELD
Lanham • Boulder • New York • London

· Published by Rowman & Littlefield
An imprint of The Rowman & Littlefield Publishing Group, Inc.
4501 Forbes Boulevard, Suite 200, Lanham, Maryland 20706
https://rowman.com

6 Tinworth Street, London SE11 5AL, United Kingdom

British Library Cataloguing in Publication Information Available

Library of Congress Cataloging-in-Publication Data

Includes bibliographic references and index.
ISBN 978-1-4758-5269-1 (cloth : alk. paper)
ISBN 978-1-4758-5270-7 (pbk. : alk. paper)
ISBN 978-1-4758-5271-4 (Electronic)

∞ ™ The paper used in this publication meets the minimum requirements of American National Standard for Information Sciences Permanence of Paper for Printed Library Materials, ANSI/NISO Z39.48-1992.

This book is dedicated to my brother, Dan Johnson, who continues to learn at successively higher levels.

Contents

Part V: Transformative Learning Theories

Part VI: Algorithmic Views of Teaching and Learning

Preface

This book describes essential learning theories and how they are applied in a teaching and learning situation. It was written with three specific audiences in mind:

1. **Practicing teachers.** If you are a practicing teacher, you may recognize many of these theories from an educational psychology course taken as part of your teacher preparation program. Back then, it is likely that these ideas may have seemed abstract and far removed from what you would need to be an effective classroom teacher. Now that you have been immersed in an authentic teaching situation, it is good to revisit these theories. You will find that you will now have a much deeper understanding of these theories and will be able to see many more possible applications.
2. **Preservice teachers.** If you are a preservice teacher, you may be taking a course related to educational psychology. Most educational psychology textbooks contain far more information than could possibly be learned in any meaningful way in a single semester by human beings who are encountering these ideas for the first time. As well, most educational psychology textbooks are expensive and contain far more "extras" and "supplementary" material than needed. This book describes just the basic essence of these theories, using as few words as possible and a limited amount of academic jargon. This will enable you to quickly understand the salient elements of these theories.
3. **Decision-makers.** Finally, if you are a school administrator, school board member, legislator, or anybody involved in making decisions related to schools or classrooms, this book can help you make better decisions. Too often, regulations, mandates, laws, standards, policies,

or important decisions about what goes on inside a school or class-room are based on people's own experience as students. This kind of decision is called an "I-think-isms." An I-think-ism is something that you think to be true or what seems to make good sense but is not supported by research or research-based theories. Neither of these are a good basis for educational decision-making.

VIDEO MINILECTURES

There are minilectures related to the content found in each chapter. These minilectures are between two and eight minutes in duration and organized by chapter. If you are a student, they can be used to help you understand the content. If you are an instructor, please feel free to use them for online or hybrid courses. These can be found at www.OPDT-Johnson.com.

Part I

Background

Chapter 1 provides background information related to theories, learning, and becoming an expert teacher.

- Chapter 1: Theories, Learning, and Learning to Teach

Chapter One

Theories, Learning, and Learning to Teach

THEORIES

In the chapters that follow, you will encounter several different learning theories. The word *theory* is often associated with an untested idea or an unsupported supposition. It is also used to describe one's conception about how things work. However, when used in an educational or scientific context, the definition of a theory is a bit more precise. Here a theory is a way to explain a set of facts. Put another way, if reality were a dot-to-dot picture, a theory would be a way to connect a set of data dots. Each of the data dots in this picture is created by research.

Accepted theories connect a wide array of data dots. These theories have been confirmed through a variety of different types of research studies and observations conducted over time. Accepted theories are then used to understand, predict, and describe phenomena. They can also be used to support existing practices or as the basis for designing new ones.

Different theories connect different data dots in different ways, resulting in a variety of theoretical pictures, each advocating slightly different practices and practical applications. As well, there is often considerable overlap between theories. You will see this overlap when you encounter slightly different versions of the same idea described in various places.

LEARNING

Described here are five general observations about learning and humans. Many of these ideas are described in various form from different theoretical perspectives in the chapters that follow.

1. **Learning is something humans do from the moment of birth to their last days.** As babies, we learn to associate certain stimuli with pleasurable experiences and other stimuli with less pleasurable experiences. Throughout our lives, we are constantly interacting with stimuli (both internal and external). These many and varied stimuli help us form associations, add knowledge to the file cabinets in our heads, strengthen neural pathways, develop new insights, and generate new ideas.

2. **Humans are naturally inclined to learn.** Our big human brains are hardwired to acquire knowledge and to understand phenomena. We are curious creatures who inherently try to make sense of the world that confronts us. It is this natural inclination that has enabled our species to evolve from early times. Teaching is effortless when we are able to align learning experiences with this natural inclination. It is much harder when what and how we teach are not aligned with this natural inclination.

3. **Human learning is effortless if the material to be learned is interesting or relevant.** If learners actually want to learn what is being taught, teaching is effortless, and learning is easy. Using learning material that is perceived to be meaningless, boring, or irrelevant makes teaching and learning more difficult. Learning material can be made relevant by connecting it to learners' needs or personal interests or by presenting the learning material in ways that are compelling or amusing or that arouse curiosity.

4. **Human learning is effortless if instruction is aligned with how humans learn.** Humans learn through play, application, conversation, social interaction, exploration, trial and error, discovery, experience, inquiry, and a variety of other ways.

5. **Human learning is cyclical not linear.** Humans learn things by revisiting them many times at successively higher levels. You cannot present information just once and expect them to have learned it. Humans need to revisit skills and concepts several times and in different circumstances. With each visit, we learn at increasingly higher levels.

BEING AND BECOMING AN EXPERT TEACHER

It is naïve to think that a finished teaching product can be created in four semesters of any teacher preparation program. These programs instead provide the knowledge and skills for preservice teachers to begin their journey toward being and becoming skillful professionals and, eventually, expert teachers.

A body of knowledge is an essential component of being and becoming an expert in any domain (Sternberg and Williams, 2010). There are four kinds of knowledge necessary for teaching expertise: pedagogical knowledge, pedagogical content knowledge, content knowledge, and knowledge of learners and learning (Bruer, 1999; Darling-Hammond, 1999; Eggen and Kauchak, 2007).

- **Pedagogical knowledge.** This is knowledge of general teaching strategies used to impart information, teach skills, or enhance learning in all subject areas. This includes strategies such as cooperative learning, expository teaching, discovery learning, problem-based learning, inquiry, universal design for learning, and various forms of multilevel instruction (Johnson, 2017). Expert teachers have a toolbox filled with an assortment of these strategies that can be used with a variety of students in a variety of situations.
- **Pedagogical content knowledge.** This is knowledge of teaching strategies used to teach specific content or skills. For example, expert teachers know the best strategies for teaching reading (Johnson, 2016), science, math, writing, or other content areas.
- **Content knowledge.** This is a body of knowledge related to the subject matter that is to be taught. Expert teachers have subject area expertise. For example, math teachers know a lot about math, social studies teachers know a lot about social studies, and so on. This body of knowledge guides the expert teacher in deciding what is taught and in what order. Expert elementary and special education teachers often are required to have expertise in a variety of areas.
- **Knowledge of learners and learning.** This is knowledge of the learning process, learning theories, and human development as it relates to social, emotional, intellectual, moral, and personal development. Expert teachers know about their students and how these students best learn. This book is designed to help increase your understanding of this type of knowledge.

Part II

Neurological Learning Theory

Chapters 2 and 3 examine neurological learning theory. This theory describes the function of the brain as learning occurs. From this perspective, learning is making new neural pathways, strengthening neural pathways, creating new neural networks, or expanding existing neural networks.

- Chapter 2: Neurological Learning Theory
- Chapter 3: Applying Neurological Learning Theory

Chapter Two

Neurological Learning Theory

LEARNING AND THE BRAIN

The brain is our learning organ. The human brain has three parts: the brain stem, the cerebellum, and the cerebrum. The *brain stem*, sometimes called the reptilian brain or lower brain, is the oldest most primitive part of the human brain. It regulates our life support systems and things within our body that do not take conscious thought.

The *cerebellum* is a small part of the brain that plays an important role in motor control. It takes input from other parts of the brain, the spinal cord, and sensory receptors, to coordinate the movements of the muscles and skeleton.

The *cerebrum* is the largest part of the brain; it is covered by a thin layer called the *cerebral cortex*. This is responsible for the higher cognitive functions such as thinking, reasoning, imagination, decision-making, and problem-solving. The cerebral cortex is divided into four sections called lobes. Each lobe is associated with certain types of thinking:

- Frontal lobe: reasoning, decision-making, emotions, problem-solving, and parts of speech
- Parietal lobe: movement, perception of stimuli, taste, recognition, and orientation
- Occipital lobe: visual processing
- Temporal lobe: memory, speech, and perception and recognition of auditory stimuli

An Integrated Whole

There are two halves, or hemispheres, to the brain that are connected by the *corpus callosum*. Each side of the brain has some specialization; however,

9

the brain works holistically. That is, the two sides work as an integrated whole communicating back and forth. Thus, while people may be better able to process certain types of data, there are no such things as left-brained or right-brained people. In the same way, while there are certain areas of the brain that seem to specialize in certain types of tasks, there are not specific parts that are completely responsible for any one function. Instead, thinking is distributed across many areas of the brain.

Creating Neural Networks

Most of what we call thinking and learning occurs in the cerebrum, specifically the cerebral cortex, where there are billions of brain cells called *neurons*. Each neuron is like a minicomputer that transmits and receives electrochemical signals in the form of nerve impulses. Each neuron can send up to fifty thousand messages per minute. Multiply this by the one hundred billion to two hundred billion neurons in our brains, and you begin to understand the power of this human-brain-computing-device.

From a neurological perspective, learning of any kind is a matter creating neural networks and strengthening neural pathways. When stimuli in the external world are perceived, relevant sense organs send signals to various part of our brain where neurons are stimulated. (Neurons can also be stimulated by other neurons as well. For example, the very act of thinking stimulates neurons and related neurons.) Once stimulated, a signal in the form of an electrical impulse is sent down a long fiber of the individual neuron called an *axon* (see figure 2.1). At the end of the axon there is a gap, called a *synapse*, that separates the neurons. Here the electrical impulse triggers a chemical release (*neurotransmitter*) that crosses the gap. The neurotransmissions are received on the other side of the gap by *neuroreceptors*, found at the end of a shorter, branching fiber of another neuron called a *dendrite*. The dendrite brings the signal up to the neuron. The signal then continues its journey down the axon to the next neuron and beyond.

Stimulated neurons automatically send and receive messages to and from all the surrounding or related neurons. As new neurons become linked up, *neural pathways* are created, existing pathways are strengthened, and more sophistical webs or *neural networks* are formed (see figure 2.2). These neural networks facilitate the processing of new and related information. In other words, new learning and experiences create new and more expansive neural networks, making it easier to make connections with other new and related information and experiences. These neural networks represent the information in the head that is used to make sense of new information. Thus, learning begets more learning. The more we learn, the easier it becomes to learn more.

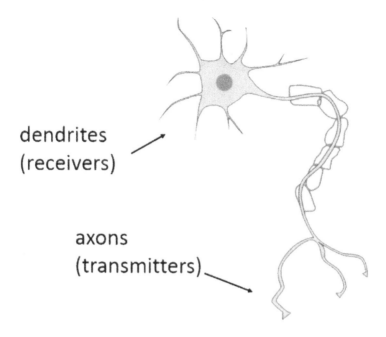

dendrites
(receivers)

axons
(transmitters)

Figure 2.1.   Neuron. https://www.vectorstock.com/royalty-free-vector/a-single-neuron-vector-20206887.

We Create Our Own Reality

At birth, billions of neurons exist in our brain like a gigantic dot-to-dot picture; but for the most part the dots are not connected and there are no preconceived pictures. As we begin receiving various stimuli from the physical environment, neurons fire and become connected with other neurons to form intercommunicating neural networks. The dots begin to connect and form our ever-evolving picture of reality. As already stated, these neural networks help us to perceive and process new information from the world around us. Thus, how we interpret and perceive reality is determined by our past experiences. Since each person's neural networks are unique to that person and his or her experiences, each person has a slightly different picture of reality. This means that there can be no such thing as a completely objective view of reality, because even the most objective accounts of data are still subjected to a very subjective interpretation.

As we act upon the world, the world in turn acts upon us in the form of new neural pathways and neural networks. In this way, learning actually changes the physical structure of the brain as new neural networks are formed. The term for this is *neural plasticity*. It refers to the brain's ability to

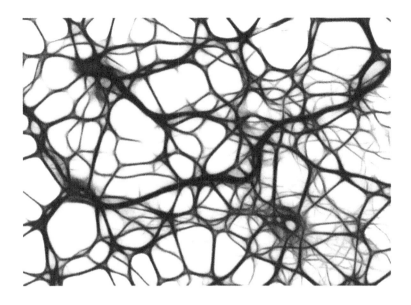

Figure 2.2.   Neural network. https://pixabay.com/ (royalty free).

organize and reorganize itself by forming new neural connections throughout a person's life.

   Right now, you are reading about the human brain. You most likely have had some exposure to information related to this. These related neural networks are sending mild electrochemical impulses back and forth in your brain. As you pick up new bits of information from this chapter, these networks connect with other neurons and expand. The dot-to-dot picture grows with more lines connecting to more dots. You are seeing how one thing is associated with another and connections between other neural networks are formed. And as you continue to visit this network with new and related bits of information, the pathways between neurons become wider as more neurons are connected into the network. And as you are striving to make sense of this chapter, connecting new information to known information, and incorporating your own experiences, your brain is changing. This change will make comprehending a little bit easier the next time you read something about learning and the brain.

Two-Way Flow

As data are taken in from the eyes and ears, they move to the relay station in the brain called the *thalamus*. The thalamus receives and initially processes sense data before they move to the cortex. The cortex is the part of the brain responsible for higher thinking and memory.

However, information does not flow just one way from the senses up to the cortex (bottom-up). Brain imaging research shows that as we perceive and process data taken in by the various senses, information flows from the cortex down to the thalamus (top-down) as well as from the thalamus up to the cortex (Hawkins, 2004). In fact, there is almost ten times more information flowing down from the cortex to the thalamus (corticothalamic connections) than up from the thalamus to the cortex (thalamocortical connections) (Strauss, 2014). This top-down flow of information is used to enable us to interpret and come to understand reality (see figure 2.3).

In order for your brain to function efficiently, data contained in our neural networks are used to reach out and make predictions about what we are about to perceive, experience, or encounter. Sense data are then used to confirm, revise, or deconstruct these predictions and construct our current view of reality. For example, if you are about to enter a restaurant, your brain has already made predictions as to what this restaurant will look like based on the all restaurants you have experienced in your life. You do not have to relearn the concepts of restaurants and what to do every time you go to a different restaurant. This restaurant data exist in your neural network and are connected to all other related restaurant concepts and experiences. This is used to

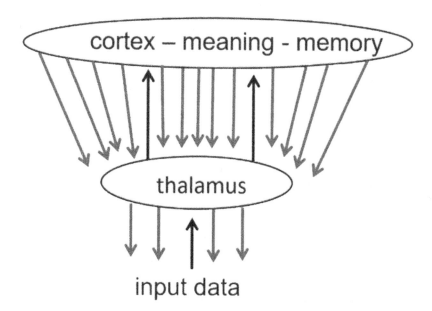

Figure 2.3.   Two-way flow of information.

help you understand what you are experiencing and predict what you are about to experience.

PERCEPTION AND MEMORY

Perception is the meaning or interpretation our brain imposes on the stimuli to which we have attended. Attention precedes perception. We first attend to the particular stimuli that we are sensing, then perception occurs when our brain imposes meaning on it.

Perception Is a Two-Way Street

When you take a picture with a digital camera, the aperture opens very briefly. The light waves, traveling through space, squeeze through the aperture and hit a sensor chip that then breaks them into millions of pixels to create an exact replica of the image before it. That image will be stored as a picture for a very long time. If you uploaded that picture from your camera or computer after many years, it would look exactly the same as when it was first stored.

However, the human brain is not a camera. Perception is not purely a bottom-up process that moves one direction from stimuli to perception to memory. Instead, the information contained in our neural networks is used to help us perceive things in the external world. In other words, once we perceive a familiar pattern in the external world, our brain fills in the blanks with the information contained in our neural networks. This is a much more efficient process than trying to constantly construct reality every moment using only sense data. And the more knowledge contained in our neural networks related to the object of our perception, the less we need to rely on sense data to perceive the object.

To illustrate, imagine you are driving down a dirt road in the middle of a forest. You stop and get out of your car. You see a partial shape of something large and dark, you see movement, and you hear some low growling sounds. All these stimuli have bear-like qualities. You would not have to wait until you had all the external bear data to determine that there was a bear present. This would take far too long, and you would probably be eaten during the interim. Instead, you use the knowledge in your neural network to fill in the blanks using as little external information as possible. You instantly perceive the bear and realize you need to get back into your car.

Your brain not only perceives things based on limited external data, it also organizes elements of the environment into objects even when not all the data are present. This is called *perceptual organization*. The natural tendency for your brain to perceive patterns in the environment is called *Gestalt*. This is a German word that refers to completing a pattern or configuration based on partial data. Gestalt can also be thought of as a filling in the blanks.

Seeing with Our Brain

As previously stated, perception is interpreting stimuli or creating meaning with external stimuli. The brain is the organ used to create meaning. Thus, we perceive things with our brain, not our eyes or other sense organs. This section examines how your eyes and brain work together to paint a picture on the canvas of your mind.

When we look at things, our eyes do not maintain a steady gaze. If you look at a picture and attend to the movement of your eyes, you will notice that your eyes flitter about like a hummingbird. If you try to keep your eyes perfectly still and focus on one element, everything around that element soon starts to get fuzzy and eventually disappears. Our eyes perceive things by moving about. Instead of one large picture, your brain is constantly taking very small snapshots to create a picture.

One reason why your eyes need to dart about is that you only have a small window of precise, clear vision when you peer out upon the world. This small window is called the *foveal*. It is about the size of a grape held at arm's length. If your eyes did not constantly move, you would have a very tiny view of the world. The area of vision around the foveal is called the *parafoveal*. This is about the size of an orange held at arm's length; data here are somewhat fuzzy and unfocused. All else is called *periphery*; data here are very unclear. Without knowledge of your surroundings, it would be impossible to distinguish the images found here. However, your brain gives you the impression that you see everything clearly, when in fact you create a movie in your head by taking a series of tiny snapshots and filling in the blanks.

Memory

Why is it that people sometimes remember the same thing differently? Three reasons: First, as stated previously, you use your neural networks to perceive and interpret things in the external world. Since our neural networks are created by our individual experiences, no two people perceive and interpret things in exactly the same way. So, even if two people have the same experience, they perceive it in slightly different ways. This means they also remember it differently.

Second, in order to operate efficiently, our brain stores only the salient elements of things perceived and experienced. In other words, memory is stored in a form that captures the essential relationships or patterns, but not the details (Hawkins, 2004). So, as you recall things from memory, you retrieve just the salient elements of the actual thing and your brain fills in the blanks with related things in your neural network. In this sense, memory is never an exact replication of reality. There is always a constructed element to it. The things retrieved from memory have also been influenced by other things in your neural network. And the more distant the memory, the more things there are in your neural network to influence it.

And third, both memory and perception are influenced by our emotions (Purves et al., 2012). Emotions affect how things are interpreted when they are first perceived. Emotions also influence how things are interpreted when they are recalled.

Chapter Three

Applying Neurological Learning Theory

This chapter expands upon and examines some of the implications and applications of neurological learning theory described in the chapter 2.

LEARNING

As stated in the chapter 2, accumulated knowledge is stored in the neural networks in our cortex. These are like three dimensional dot-to-dot pictures that continually change with new experience and encounters. Learning, from a neurological perspective, is a matter strengthening neural pathways, creating new neural networks, or expanding existing neural networks. Based on this, five implications for teaching and learning are described here.

1. **The importance of knowledge.** Humans use their neural networks to make sense of phenomena and to learn new things. As such, an important part of our jobs as teachers is to present a well-organized body of knowledge to students and to create experiences that enable them to develop and expand their neural networks. A body of knowledge is a critical part of achievement in any area (Ormrod, 2012). In fact, one of the differences between novices and experts is in their knowledge. Experts have more if it that is better organized; novices have less of it that is not well organized. Knowledge enhances problem-solving, decision-making, reading fluency, comprehension, and the ability to learn new things (see chapter 12).
2. **School readiness programs.** Students who enter school with limited enrichment experiences, exploration activities, conversational oppor-

tunities, and exposure to books often have neural networks that are not as well developed as their peers. As such, they often have a harder time learning school-related things when compared to their peers. School readiness programs such as Head Start or Early Start have been shown to be effective in closing some of these gaps (Aikins, Klein, Tarullo, and West, 2013).

3. **Teacher knowledge.** A continually developing knowledge base is also important for teachers. Chapter 1 described the four types of knowledge possessed by expert teachers: content knowledge, pedagogical knowledge, pedagogical content knowledge, and knowledge of learners and learning. Expert teachers use this knowledge to perceive and understand events in their classrooms, diagnose learning problems, design effective learning experiences, and make good educational decisions. Thus, professional growth and development opportunities that enable teachers to develop their knowledge in these areas is essential for improving the quality of education students receive. It also enables the field of education to continue to evolve.

4. **Connect the new to the known.** Learning is enhanced when teachers help students connect new information to what they already know. When introducing new skills or concepts, you should build upon existing neural networks. At the beginning of a lesson, describe or remind students of related things they already know. During the lesson have students show how the new thing relates to known things. And when describing new skills and concepts, use terms and concepts with which students are familiar.

5. **Use prereading activities.** Students' ability to read and understand their textbooks is enhanced by providing sufficient knowledge before reading. There are two things you can do here: First, you can preteach important ideas or concepts before asking students to read about them. Second, you can present the lecture, activity, or experience first, and then ask students to read about it later. Very rarely should students be asked to read a text or chapter cold (without any prereading activity).

TEACHING WITH THE BRAIN IN MIND

In the book *Teaching with the Brain in Mind*, Eric Jensen (2005) outlined seven critical factors that should be addressed in effective teaching: (a) engagement, (b) repetition, (c) input quantity, (d) coherence, (e) timing, (f) error corrections, and (g) emotional states. Each of these is described here.

Engagement

Learning is most efficient when students are engaged in ways that results in focused attention. Four tips for enhancing focused attention:

- Reduce the length of time required for focused attention during instruction. Human attention is a limited. Thus, instruction in which students are asked to passively absorb information should be limited. For the primary grades this duration should be five to eight minutes; for middle school and high school students, twelve to fifteen minutes (see chapter 15). Outside of this, learning is reduced significantly. This does not mean the total lesson should be restricted to these durations; instead, direct instruction within those lessons should be broken into segments of these durations followed by activities that get students actively involved. This activity could be as simple as, "Think of one idea that seems to stick in your head and share with a neighbor."
- Include the least amount instruction necessary. Students do not learn by listening to you tell them things. To the greatest extent possible, create the conditions for authentic learning experiences (see chapter 19) and then get out of the way.
- Use relevant tasks and activities. Design learning experiences in which students are able to read, explore, and discuss issues that have personal meaning or that are connected to their lives in some way.
- Provide time and space for students to become engrossed in learning. Block scheduling is effective with older students. For younger students, once they have become engaged in the act of learning, leave them alone. Resist the need to move on.

Repetition

Human brains are not like computers where you input data once and it is stored and retrieved exactly as you inputted it. Human brains need to touch skills and concepts repeatedly over time in order strengthen neural pathways and build neural networks. Two tips:

- Use prelesson activities that give students a sense of what they will learn. Use post-lesson or independent activities in which students are engaged with the salient elements of what they have just learned. These are both forms of repetition.
- Review, revisit, and reinforce often. You cannot teach a skill or concept once and expect student mastery. You must review and revisit skills and concepts many times, in different ways, at successively higher levels over time for real learning to occur.

Input Quantity

The brain can learn a lot over time but only a little at a time. Five tips:

- Use chunks vs. blobs. It is much easier to process and encode new information when it is presented in small, meaningful chunks rather than large
  blobs.
- Allow adequate time for learning. In-depth learning requires time for organizing, integrating, and storing new information.
- Use distributed practice. Students are more apt to stay fully engaged and
  will learn more if complex instruction is distributed over time rather than
  crammed into a single session (see chapter 11). For example, providing
  fifteen minutes of instructional input in three five-minute segments dis-
  persed over twenty minutes is more effective for younger children than
  fifteen minutes of massed instructional input followed by five minutes of
  down time.
- Insert pause and process (P&P) time into instruction. Instead of constant
  exposure to a single instructional element, use brief bits of instruction or
  instructional activities with small bits of P&P time. Students need this
  break to think about and fully process the instructional input. Inserting
  small breaks into your lesson will enable students to engage all parts of the
  brain and to integrate new information with knowledge already stored in
  neural networks. Effective P&P is intentional and planned.
- Slow down but move quickly from one thing to the next. This is not as
  paradoxical as it sounds. Your actual instruction should be at a pace at
  which students can fully understand and process the content. This sometimes means including less content in each instructional session. But if
  you spend too much time on a single thing, students will become bored
  and disengage. This means you need to watch your students and move
  quickly from one thing to the next thing when you sense they are ready to
  move on.

Coherence

As will be described in several places in this book, our brain naturally tries to
see patterns and make sense out of the world we encounter. It strives to find
logical consistency in all the stimuli that bombards us at any given moment.
Three tips:

- Show students the structure of what is to be learned using advanced orga-
  nizers (see chapter 15).
- Connect the new to the known (as discussed earlier).
- Design lessons that are organized with structure and coherence.

Timing

Our brains do not operate at peak efficiency all the time. Instead we have peaks and valleys throughout the day. Four tips:

- Expect students' performance to vary from day to day and even within the day.
- Teach students about their brains. Let them know that there may be times during the day when it is more difficult to study and learn.
- Brains need sleep to operate efficiently. Adolescents especially tend to be sleep deprived. Communicate frequently with parents about the importance of their children getting enough sleep.
- Use activity shifts, movement, and stand and stretch breaks within the teaching/learning session to stimulate the brain.

Error Correction

Trial-and-error learning is how our brain learns best. Hence, humans need to be able to mess around, get feedback, and make corrections. Inquiry, discovery, and experiential learning are all strategies or approaches that allow for this. (see chapters 14 and 19).

Emotional States

Students' emotional states are a significant variable for learning (Jensen, 2003). Positive emotional states enhance learning. Negative emotional states detract from learning. Strive to create positive states in which students are motivated or want to learn. Four tips:

- Reduce the threat of failure or embarrassment.
- Use scaffolding to enable students to experience success (see chapter 9).
- Include games and other fun activities to create positive emotional states. Games can reinforce learning and at the same time create positive emotional states. You can end each teaching session with a game or something fun so that students have something to look forward to.
- Include social interaction. We are a social species. Our brains evolved to interact with other humans. Use this natural inclination by including activities in which students interact with other students.

READING

Understanding the basic process of how the brain learns and creates meaning will enable teachers at all levels to design effective reading experiences and instruction for students.

A Phonological Processing Model of Reading

Traditionally it was thought that reading was simply sounding out words. Here the reader put sounds to symbols on the page, then put the sound-symbols together to create words, and finally put the words together to create ideas. It was assumed that these ideas would flow one way, from the page, to the thalamus, and up to the cortex. This is called a bottom-up view of reading based on the *phonological processing model*. However, this model is part of an incomplete theory of reading because it does not account for some important facts:

1. Proficient readers do not look at all the words on the page (Paulson, 2005; Weaver, 2009). This tells us that readers are using more than the words and letters on the page to create meaning. They are using background knowledge as well as semantic and syntactic information to fill in the blanks as they read (see 2).
2. When reading, proficient readers often insert words that are not in the text but are semantically or syntactically correct (Paulson, 2005). Again, this demonstrates that proficient readers do not notice and process every word, that information other than what is on the page is being used to construct meaning.
3. As described in the last chapter, the ratio of corticothalamic nerve fibers to the thalamocortical fibers is ten to one (Hawkins, 2004; Strauss, 2014). This means that during the act of reading, almost ten times more information flows from the cortex down to the thalamus than flows up from the page to the thalamus, and then up to the cortex. This tells us that information contained in our neural networks is being used along with text clues to create meaning.
4. During reading, eye movement is not based on what is on the page; instead, information from the cortex is used to direct the eyes (Rayner, Liversedge, White, and Vergilino-Perez, 2003). In other words, higher level thinking processes drive or mediate lower level word recognition processes (Paulson and Freeman, 2003; Straus 2011).

A Neurocognitive Model of Reading

A *neurocognitive model of reading* (based on neurological learning theory) recognizes the meaning-making function of the brain. According to this model, reading is defined as creating meaning with print, not simply sounding out words. During this meaning-making process, the knowledge stored in our cortex is used to constantly reach out and predict the meanings of words in the sentences we are about to read (Goodman, Fries, and Strauss, 2016). Cueing systems provide the brain clues (or cues) as to what the word or sentence might be (Johnson, 2016). Our brain uses three cuing systems to make these predications:

1. **Semantic cueing system.** Semantics refers to meaning. As you read, you use context and background knowledge to recognize words and predict what the next word might be. The semantic cueing system is the most efficient of the three in terms of speed and space required in working memory to recognize words.
2. **Syntactic cueing system.** Syntax has to do with the grammatical structure of the language. As your brain reads, you also use your knowledge of grammar, sentence structure, word order, tense and plurality, prefixes and suffixes, nouns and verbs, and function words (prepositions, pronouns, and so on) to recognize words. This is the second most efficient cueing system.
3. **Grapho-phonetic cueing system.** *Grapho* refers to symbols, *phono* refers to sounds. The grapho-phonetic cueing systems uses letter sounds to predict what the next word might be. Of the three cueing systems, this one is the least efficient because it focuses on individual letters and letter patterns instead of words and ideas. As you will see in chapter 10, working memory has a very limited capacity. In creating meaning with print, it is more efficient and effective to use words and ideas vs. individual letters.

Your Dancing Eyeballs

In chapter 2 we looked at how your eyes function when perceiving things in general. Here we will look at eye movement during reading. As you read this page your eyes are not moving from left to right, letter to letter, word to word in a straight, steady line. Your brain simply gives the impression that they do. Eye movement research shows that your eyes move unevenly across the page, going back occasionally, skipping some words, and fixating on others (Paulson and Goodman, 2011). The small, rapid, jerky movements that your eyes make are called *saccades.* Where your eyes stop is called a *fixation.* A *regression* is when your eye goes back to check on a word.

While reading, your eyes fixate on only about 60 percent of the words you read (Paulson and Goodman, 2008). With unfamiliar reading material, you fixate on more words; with familiar material, you fixate on fewer words. This means your eyes skip over 40 percent of the words on the page. It only appears as if you are reading every word because your brain fills in the blanks. This again is consistent with the neurocognitive model of reading. Reading instruction that only focuses on individual letters can actually impede reading progress. Thus, instruction on letter sounds (phonics) should always be provided along with instruction and activities that develop semantic and syntactic cueing systems (Johnson, 2016).

Chapter 2 described three visual regions: foveal, parafoveal, and peripheral. This is how they apply to reading: The *foveal*, the point of fixation where you are able to see clearly and process details, enables you to perceive only about three to six letters. The *parafoveal*, the region directly surrounding the foveal region, enables you to perceive about twenty-four to thirty letters, but not very clearly. Without some sort of context, the strings of letters here are indistinguishable. The *peripheral* region is everything else. Here you are able to perceive only gross shapes but not individual letters.

Considering this very small in-focus viewing area, how is anybody able to read more than ten words per minute? We are able to read quickly because of the top-down flow of information as described in chapter 2. We use the information contained in our neural networks, along with the context of what we are reading (semantics), as well as grammar and word order (syntax) to make predictions about the upcoming text. These predictions enable us to make sense of the semi-blurred letters found in the parafoveal regions and to quickly recognize words as we are reading. If we are reading efficiently, we do not process every letter in a word or every word in a sentence; rather we recognize words using semantics, syntax, and minimal letter clues. Because we are creating meaning with print, our brain only tricks us into thinking we have looked at every letter in every word.

The implications: First, reading instruction must include activities to develop all three cueing systems (Johnson, 2016). And also, when students come to a word that they do not recognize, there is a tendency to ask them to sound it out. This is often the worst advice, as it gets them focusing on individual letters instead of meaning. Using semantic and syntactic clues is much more efficient and effective (Johnson, 2016). When students come to a word that they do not recognize, you should instead ask, "What word makes sense?"

DIFFERENT VIEWS, VALUES,
AND TEACHING PHILOSOPHIES

Neurological learning theory can also explain how is it that people have such widely varying views on important issues related to education (and other areas). As described several times in chapter 2, we each use our own unique interconnected series of neural networks to perceive reality and make sense of the world. Since our neural networks are formed by our individual experiences, no two people have identical networks; hence, no two people perceive things in exactly the same way. This is why people of good character can have widely differing views on policies and practices related to education.

There is a natural impulse to initially discredit and reject views that do not align with our current way of thinking. However, it is only by considering a variety of ideas that we are able to expand our neural networks and continue to evolve as both teachers and human beings.

Part III

Behavioral Learning Theories

Chapters 4 to 7 examine behavioral learning theory. These theories share a common view of learning. From this perspective, learning is a relatively permanent change in behavior (or behavioral potentiality) that occurs as a result of experience.

- Chapter 4: Behaviorism—Classical Conditioning
- Chapter 5: Behaviorism—Operant Conditioning
- Chapter 6: Applying Behavioral Learning Theories in the Classroom
- Chapter 7: Social Cognitive Learning Theory

Chapter Four

Behaviorism — Classical Conditioning

A BEHAVIORAL VIEW OF LEARNING

Behavioral learning theories describe learning as a relatively permanent change in behavior (or behavioral potentiality) that occurs as a result of experience (Hergenhahn and Olson, 2005). Classical conditioning (sometimes called associative learning) is described in this chapter. Operant conditioning (sometimes called instrumental conditioning) is described in chapter 5.

CLASSICAL CONDITIONING

The essence of classical condition is this: If two stimuli occur together frequently enough, they eventually become associated with each other (Johnson, 2013). The result of this association is that each stimulus eventually produces a similar response. For example, let us imagine that you hated prune juice so much that drinking it caused you to gag. If a buzzer sounded each time you drank prune juice, and if this was repeated many times, eventually just the sound of the buzzer would cause a similar physical reaction (gagging). Learning then would be a matter of strengthening the bond between the two stimuli (prune juice and the buzzer) so that each would elicit the same response (gagging).

Originally, classical conditioning focused only on reflexive behaviors such as gagging or the salivation reflex of Pavlov's dog (which will be described). More recently, classical conditioning has included voluntary responses to conditioned stimuli as well as emotions and internal states.

Ivan Pavlov

The discovery of classical conditioning was made by Ivan Pavlov (1849–1936), a Russian physiologist studying the digestive system in dogs. One day he was collecting dogs' saliva to measure the amount of salivation produced when the dogs smelled food (meat powder). He noticed (quite by accident) that not only did the dog salivate when meat powder was placed in its mouth, but also when things (or stimuli) associated with the meat powder were presented. These other stimuli included the sound of the door, the presence of the food dish, and the sight of the person who brought the meat powder.

Pavlov then conducted experiments where the meat powder was paired with the sound of a bell. Through this pairing, the dog eventually came to salivate when it heard just the sound of the bell (without meat powder). Again, this is classical conditioning. Here a stimulus (meat powder) that caused a naturally occurring or unconditioned response (salivation) was repeatedly paired with a neutral stimulus (bell). Eventually the neutral stimulus presented by itself produced the same response as the original stimulus. This response had been learned through conditioning, hence the name "conditioned response." When two things are paired together enough times, the one thing becomes associated with the other.

John Watson

While the roots of behaviorism are found in Pavlov's work, John Watson (1878–1958) is known as the founder of behaviorism. Before him, psychology was studied mainly through introspection (people examining their own thought processes and internal states). Watson brought a degree of scientific rigor to the field by moving away from the study of consciousness, to the study of behaviors. According to Watson, mental events (anything happening in the mind) could not be dealt with directly and thus should be avoided. Instead, psychology should only study behavior and the conditions that affect behavior. These were things that could be objectively observed and measured.

To Watson, personality was nothing more than a collection of conditioned reflexes. He postulated that humans had only three basic emotions: anger, fear, and love. It was through classical conditioning that these three emotions and their variations became attached to different stimuli (things, people, and experiences). To Watson, humans were merely responding organisms constantly responding to various stimuli in their environment. Over time certain reflexive patterns became reinforced through classical conditioning. According to Watson the variability in people was simply a result of their varied experiences.

In 1920 Watson conducted an experiment involving an eleven-month-old child named Albert. Before the experiment, Albert was presented with a white rat. He showed no fear of the rat, reaching out to touch it when he saw it. During the initial part of the experiment, Albert was presented with the rat and again reached for it. As soon as he touched it, a researcher directly behind Albert hit a steel bar with a hammer. This made a very loud noise, causing Albert to jump, fall forward, and cry. This was repeated several times. Eventually, when the rat was presented to Albert he would fall over, begin to cry, and try to crawl away. Watson concluded that an emotional response (fear) could be taught through conditioning. Conditioning, according to Watson, occurred because of the close succession of events (Watson and Rayner, 1920). The more often they occurred closely together, the stronger the association became. This is known as the principle of contiguity.

TERMS AND CONCEPTS RELATED TO CLASSICAL CONDITIONING

The following terms and concepts are related to classical conditioning.

- **Classical conditioning.** Pairing one thing with another to produce a similar response.
- **Unconditioned stimulus.** A thing or event that evokes a physiological or emotional response.
- **Unconditioned response.** A naturally occurring response to an unconditioned stimulus.
- **Neutral stimulus.** A thing or event not connected to a response.
- **Conditioned stimulus.** A neutral stimulus that evokes a response only after conditioning.
- **Conditioned response.** A learned response to a previously neutral stimulus.
- **Principle of contiguity.** Two things followed closely that eventually become associated with each other.
- **Generalization.** A response to stimuli that are similar to the unconditioned stimulus. Here an organism that has been conditioned to respond to a conditioned stimulus also responds to similar or related stimuli. Using Pavlov's experiment, the dog would initially respond to a particular bell. Generalization would occur when the dog learned to respond to sounds similar to the bell sound.
- **Aversive conditioning.** Pairing something unpleasant (an aversive stimulus) with a particular situation.

APPLICATIONS

Theories do not predict human behavior; they help us understand human behavior. Classical conditioning helps us understand why human beings sometimes react the way they do to conditions, events, or things even when the connection seems unrelated. So, how might we apply this theory to our classrooms? Two tips:

- **Create a positive, nurturing presence.** Watson demonstrated that classical conditioning can affect a person's emotional state. Humans think and emote with the same brain; hence, emotions affect learning. Positive emotions enhance learning, negative emotions impede learning. Thus, your demeanor and ways in which you respond to students and colleagues affect the effectiveness of your teaching and the degree of learning that occurs. Children tend to have positive emotional responses to warm, nurturing teachers. If school becomes associated with a warm, nurturing teacher, children will be more relaxed and less anxious than they would if it were associated with a cold, demanding teacher.
- **Eliminate failure, frustration, and humiliation.** Children with learning disabilities often experience failure and humiliation at school. They become anxious, tense, and angry in classroom learning situations. Eventually, school and everything related has the same negative effect and school becomes a very depressing place. This does not mean that students need to succeed at everything they do; instead, not succeeding or missing the mark should not be seen as a failure.

MASTER TEACHERS

Teachers must do their best to pair learning with pleasurable experiences so as to avoid the negative effects of classical conditioning. Master teachers strive to make learning interesting, successful, relevant, and personal to the greatest extent possible. Knowing the basics of classical conditioning can help in understanding the forces that shape students and cause them to act and react. Master teachers also strive to design learning experiences that reflect and respect students' natural ways of learning, their curiosity, or the developmental tasks confronting them *to the greatest degree possible.*

Chapter Five

Behaviorism—Operant Conditioning

OPERANT CONDITIONING

Whereas classical conditioning involves an organism that is passive, simply responding to stimuli, *operant conditioning* involves an organism that must first act (or operate) upon the environment in some way (Johnson, 2013). Actions (or behaviors) that are followed by pleasurable outcomes (rewards) are reinforced and tend to be repeated. Actions that are followed by unpleasant outcomes (punishment) are weakened and tend not to be repeated. In other words, organisms learn certain behaviors as they act and are then rewarded or punished.

Edward Lee Thorndike

Edward Lee Thorndike's (1874–1949) learning theory came from his study of hungry cats in a cagelike box (Lattal, 1998; Johnson 2013). On the outside of the box was a fish that the cat could see and smell. On the inside of the box was a lever that, when pressed, would open the door. Sensing the fish, the cat would engage in a variety of behaviors in an attempt to open the door and get the fish. Eventually one of these behaviors (pressing the lever) would result in the door opening and the cat getting the reward (fish).

Learning for the hungry cat was a matter of making the connection between lever-pressing and door-opening. This learning was incremental not insightful, meaning that the cat was not able to gain sudden insight or make a logical connection between the action and the reward. Instead the cat made small incremental gains toward the connection. Each time the cat was put in the box, it took successively fewer tries for it to make this connection. Eventually, after many times in the box, the cat would go directly to the lever. This is called trial-and-error learning or selecting and connecting. A behavior was selected (lever-pressing) and a connection with a consequence (door-opening) was eventually made and strengthened.

Thorndike's Laws of Learning

Based on his experiments, Thorndike came up with three laws of learning.

1. **Law of effect.** The strength of a connection is influenced by the consequences of a response. An action followed by a pleasurable consequence is more likely to be repeated. Inversely, an action followed by an annoying or painful consequence is less likely to be repeated.

   Classroom example: Tammy is in sixth grade. When she acts out in class she is rewarded by the laughter and attention of her classmates (something she enjoys). This makes it more likely that she will act out in the future. If this same behavior were met with derision and social scorn by her peers, she would be less likely to act out.

2. **Law of exercise.** Connections between a stimulus and response become strengthened with practice and weakened when practice is discontinued. In other words, the more often the cat is put in the box to make the connection between lever-pressing and door-opening, the longer this behavior will be retained. However, if the cat were put in the box only once every other week, the learning it had gained would quickly recede.

   Classroom example: If Tammy had been acting out in class and getting attention since she was in first grade, her silly behaviors would continue long after she stopped getting reinforced. If she just recently started acting out, the behavior would discontinue shortly after the rewards were discontinued.

3. **Law of readiness.** When an organism is ready to act, it is reinforcing for it to do so and annoying for is not to do so. When an organism is not ready to act, forcing it to do so is annoying.

   Classroom example: If Tammy is in a jovial mood and feels like being silly, simply being silly will be reinforcing by itself. If Tammy is in a bad mood and does not want to act out, being forced to be silly will be unpleasant even if she receives the attention she craves.

   The important educational implication for the law of readiness is that learning experiences should be aligned with students' natural tendencies and inclinations to the greatest extent possible. As described in chapter 1, learning is a natural human tendency. When students are curious and want to learn, to do so is reinforcing. When they are not ready to learn, being made to do so is painful. Students are generally not ready to learn when they are (a) forced to learn things that are irrelevant or meaningless and (b) asked to learn in ways that are not developmentally appropriate. This points to the importance of including some choice and open-ended experiences within mandated curriculums (see chapter 16). This enables students to discover and explore topics that are of interest to them.

Burrhus Frederic Skinner

B. F. Skinner (1904–1990) studied how behavior could be controlled by focusing on antecedents, behaviors, and consequences (A-B-C). The antecedent is what occurs before the behavior. This tells the organism what to do. A behavior occurs in response to the antecedent. Then, a consequence occurs (a reward or punishment) after the behavioral response, which either strengthens or weakens the behavior.

Skinner's work involved the use of a mechanism that has come to be known as a Skinner box. This was a small cage that usually had a light, a lever, and a food cup. Some Skinner boxes were also designed to elicit electric shocks via a grid in the floor. Skinner found that mice could be taught to perform specific behaviors using various reinforcement techniques. Mice were taught to press the lever (behavior) every time a light (antecedent) appeared. This lever-pressing behavior was reinforced (consequence) by a food pellet appearing in the food cup. The mouse's natural behavior was modified or changed through the use of reinforcement and punishment, hence the term *behavior modification*.

Terms

- A *reinforcer* is any consequence that increases the likelihood that a behavior will occur again. *Reinforcement* is the process of attaching reinforcers to certain behaviors. There are two types of reinforcement: positive and negative.
- *Positive reinforcement* is a reward or a pleasurable thing that is attached to a behavior. For a mouse, positive reinforcement would be the food pellet.
- *Negative reinforcement* (this term is often confused with *punishment*) is the removal of an annoying or painful condition that is attached to a behavior. If a mild electric shock was sent to a mouse through the floor of the Skinner box, negative reinforcement would be the removal of the shock that would occur by pressing the lever.
- *Immediacy* is the length of time between the behavior and the reinforcer. For reinforcement to be effective, it should occur immediately after the behavior is displayed. For example, to reinforce the lever-pressing behavior for a mouse, the food pellet needs to appear immediately upon pressing the lever.

- *Punishment* is any consequence that decreases or suppresses behavior. There are two types of punishment: presentation and removal.
- *Presentation punishment* is when an aversive stimulus (something annoying or unpleasant) follows a behavior.
- *Removal punishment* is when a rewarding stimulus is taken away following a behavior.

Limitations of Punishment

Punishment of any kind is very limited in modifying behaviors and should never be used as the *sole means* of managing behaviors. There are three reasons for this: First, whether working with mice or humans, as soon as the punishment or threat of punishment disappears, the unwanted behavior reappears. Here, the organism simply learns to avoid punishment; it does not learn the correct behavior.

Second, trying to manage behavior simply by administering punishment results in a bit of classical conditioning (aversive conditioning) whereby, for example, the school becomes paired with the aversive stimulus (punishment). This results in negative emotions that impede rather than enhance learning and eventually lead to an increase in negative behavior.

And third, by relying solely on punishment, behavior becomes controlled by external stimuli; it is never internalized. And while there may be a diminishment of problem behaviors in the short-term, this approach does little to teach the correct behavior or solve behavioral problems. As already stated, as soon as the punishment or threat of punishment disappears, the problem behaviors reappear.

Again, while there may be appropriate places for logical consequences that follow negative behaviors, punishment should not be used as the sole means of modifying behavior. If it is used, punishment should always be used in a very limited fashion and in combination with reinforcement that both teaches and rewards positive behaviors. Also, in analyzing unwanted behavior, the antecedent should always be considered as well. That is, what were the conditions that fostered the unwanted behavior? What could be done to mitigate these circumstances? One of the best ways to manage unwanted behaviors is to prevent them from occurring in the first place. This does not mean that educators should excuse unwanted behavior; instead it suggests that understanding some of the forces that may have contributed to it may enable them to be reduced or prevented.

SCHEDULES OF REINFORCEMENT

Schedules of reinforcement pertain to how, when, and how often reinforcement is given. The schedule of reinforcement determines how quickly a behavior is learned and how long it lasts (persistence) once the reinforcement disappears.

Learning and Persistence

Here are five reinforcement schedules:

1. **Continuous reinforcement** is reinforcement that is given after every behavioral response. New behaviors here are learned very quickly; however, there is little persistence. That is, once the reinforcement stops, the behavior quickly stops.

   Classroom example: Bobby is in second grade. When he comes into the classroom, he throws his coat on the floor. His teacher wants him to hang up his coat in the closet. Continuous reinforcement would be to provide a reward (positive reinforcement) each time he does this. He would very quickly learn to do this; however, as soon as the reward disappeared, the behavior would begin to fade. Also, with continuous reinforcement, the effects of the reinforcement eventually diminish over time.

2. **Fixed-interval reinforcement** is reinforcement given after specific time increments or intervals. For example, a reward would be given every ten minutes if a behavior were present. A real-life example would be a weekly quiz to reinforce reading. With fixed-interval reinforcement, the frequency of the desired behavior increases as the time for the reinforcement nears, but then drops off soon after the reinforcement is given. Also, there is little persistence once the reinforcement stops.

   Classroom example: Instead of reinforcing Bobby after every coat-hanging incident, he would get a reward for his coat-hanging behavior every two days or at the end of the week. When it was time for the reward, we would see him much more attentive to coat-hanging behavior, but soon after, his attention would lapse. If the rewards were discontinued, the desired coat-handing behavior would also soon diminish.

3. **Fixed-ratio reinforcement** is reinforcement given after a set number of behavioral responses. For example, a mouse gets a pellet after every two bar pressings or a child gets allowance money after every four dishwashing episodes. This would result in a fairly rapid increase in behavior, however, there would be little persistence. That is, when the expected reward did not occur after the defined number of responses, there would be a fairly rapid drop in behavior.

   Classroom example: To reinforce coat-hanging behavior, Bobby would be reinforced after every three coat-hanging episodes. Bobby would learn fairly quickly here with a slight lapse in attention after he earned his reward; however, there would be little persistence. His coat-hanging behavior would continue only slightly longer than the two previous reinforcement schedules after the rewards were discontinued.

4. **Variable-interval reinforcement** is reinforcement that is given after the first behavioral response and then after varying durations. A real-life example of this would be pop quizzes given to reinforce studying behaviors. The interval between reinforcement would vary (daily, every few days, or weekly). This type of reinforcement would result in a slow, steady rate of learning (students would eventually realize that they needed to study). After the reinforcement was given, there would be little reduction in the desired studying behaviors. However, after the reinforcement ceased, there would be greater persistence then the other reinforcement schedules. This means that after the reinforcement stopped, there would be a slow, steady decline of the desired studying behavior.

   Classroom example: To reinforce coat-hanging behavior, Bobby would be reinforced after the first coat-hanging incident, then his reward would be given different time intervals sometimes twice a day, sometimes every two or three days. Bobby would be slower to respond to this type of reinforcement, but the behavior would continue longer than the other reinforcement schedules once the rewards were discontinued.

5. **Variable-ratio reinforcement** is reinforcement that occurs after a varying number of behavioral responses. This is the most powerful type of reinforcement schedule for learning and maintaining behaviors. A slot machine best illustrates this type of reinforcement. Sometimes a payout comes at short intervals, sometimes longer intervals. It is unpredictable and thus keeps people coming back. What makes a slot machine even more reinforcing is that the amount or type of reward also varies. Often it is very small, occasionally it is a little bigger, and on rare occasions there is a huge payout.

   Variable-ratio reinforcement results in a rapid increase in behaviors initially with little pause after reinforcement. This type of reinforcement has the greatest persistence of all the reinforcement schedules. That is, once the reinforcement is discontinued, the response behaviors continue the longest and have the slowest amount of decline with this schedule of reinforcement.

   Classroom example: After reinforcing the first coat-hanging behavior, Bobby's teacher would begin to change the reinforcement schedule. Sometimes the reward would come after every coat-hanging behavior, sometimes after every few coat coat-hanging behaviors. When compared to continuous reinforcement, it would take slightly longer to learn this new behavior, but there would be very little decline once the rewards were discontinued.

Implications for Teaching, Learning, and Behavior Management

In order to see a new behavior appear or an old behavior disappear, use continuous reinforcement initially but soon thereafter move to a variable-ratio reinforcement schedule to maintain the behavior. To strengthen the persistence of the new behavior, slowly increase the length of time between reinforcements and decrease the frequency. Eventually you can discontinue the reinforcement. In addition, the types of rewards given should also vary.

SHAPING BEHAVIORS

Shaping occurs when new a behavior is learned by rewarding successive approximations of the desired behavior initially, followed by rewards given only after the displayed behavior becomes closer to the desired behavior. Eventually, only the full desired behavior is rewarded. For example, to use shaping to teach a chicken to dance, you would first reward the chicken every time it made a slight turn to the left. Once this behavior was learned, the chicken would then be rewarded only by making a half turn to the left. When this behavior was learned, it would be rewarded for turning a full circle. Next, it would be turning a full circle and bobbing, and on and on until the chicken eventually displayed the complete desired dancing behaviors.

Classroom example: Ms. Davis teaches a seventh-grade language arts class. During each class she assigns students a writing task and allows time for them to work on their writing assignment. However, Kevin does not use this time productively. He often jokes with his neighbors, stares off into space, draws pictures on his paper, or engages in a variety of other behaviors to avoid writing. To use shaping, Ms. Davis begins by identifying the desired behavior. In this case, it is for Kevin to begin working on his writing assignment without delay and to stay engaged. Using a token system (see chapter 6), Kevin is first rewarded for getting his paper out and putting his name on it within two minutes. After this behavior occurs on a regular basis, his reward comes only after completing this first step and then identifying a writing topic. Next, he is rewarded for completing the first two steps and two paragraphs. Then, he is rewarded for being engaged in productive writing behaviors for half the writing time. Finally, he is rewarded for being engaged in his writing task during the entire writing time.

ADDITIONAL TERMS AND CONCEPTS
RELATED TO OPERANT CONDITIONING

The following terms and concepts are also related to operant conditioning:

- **Trial and error learning** is the act of trying a number of different responses in problem-solving until a solution is found. When originally confronted with a problem, an organism will engage in multiple responses until one is found to work. In each successive attempt to solve the same problem, the number of attempts is lessened before an answer is found.
- **Incremental learning** is learning that occurs a little bit at a time rather than all at once. (With each successive problem, the number of attempts needed to arrive at the solution diminishes.)
- **Insightful learning** is learning that occurs all at once. Using logic and reasoning, humans can put things together and instantaneously make the *stimulus-response connection.*
- **Connectionism** is used to describe Thorndike's explanation of learning. He assumed learning involved the strengthening of connections between a stimulus and the response to it.
- **Transfer** is when learning that occurs in one situation is applied in a different situation. The amount of transfer is determined by the number of common elements in the two situations. As the number of common elements goes up, the amount of transfer between the two also goes up.
- **Response by analogy** is when an organism responds to similar or known situations. The response to unfamiliar situation is determined by the number of common elements in the two situations.
- **Law of conditioning**, proposed by Skinner, says that a response followed by a reinforcing stimulus is strengthened and more likely to reoccur.
- **Law of extinction**, also proposed by Skinner, says that a response that is not followed by a reinforcing stimulus is weakened and less likely to reoccur.
- **Premack Principle** is using what an organism likes to do naturally to reinforce something the organism does not like to do. Put another way, high-probability behaviors (those performed frequently under the conditions of free choice) can be used to reinforce low-probability behaviors (those that normally do not occur). For example, if a child likes to play a computer game, this can be used to reinforce something the child may not like to do, such as homework. After completing a specified amount of homework, the child would then be allowed to play on the computer.

Chapter Six

Applying Behavioral Learning Theories in the Classroom

Chapters 4 and 5 described two behavioral learning theories: classical conditioning and operant conditioning. This chapter shows how these theories might be applied in a classroom.

CLASSICAL CONDITIONING

Classical conditioning involves two stimuli being paired together many times so that eventually, when each of them occurs independently, they both produce the same response.

As we saw in John Watson's experiments with young Albert, negative emotions can be classically conditioned. This occurs in a classroom when emotions such as fear, humiliation, frustration, boredom, shame, or despair are linked with learning or school experiences (Ormrod, 2012). Eventually, school and the things to be learned there become associated with these negative emotions. As described previously, positive emotions enhance learning; negative emotions impede or disrupt learning.

Negative Emotions Related to Learning Difficulties

Negative emotions are often generated when students experience difficulties learning school-related things. Here are eight strategies that can be used to lessen this effect.

1. **Teach within the zone of proximal development.** During teaching and learning, students' independent level is the level at which they can

accomplish a task or learn independently. The frustration level is the level at which students cannot accomplish a task or learn even with teacher support (see chapter 9). The *zone of proximal development* is just above the independent level, where students can achieve success with teacher support or scaffolding (Lefrancois, 2011).

2. **Use multilevel teaching strategies.** In any classroom there will be students of varying ability levels and strength and deficit areas. Multilevel teaching strategies such as universal design for learning (UDL), workshop approaches, contract learning, and tiered instruction can be used to avoid frustrating students and help all students achieve their full potential (Johnson, 2017).

3. **Use homework to practice learning.** Homework should not be used to challenge students or as a mechanism for sorting and grading. Instead, it should be used to practice or reinforce the learning that has already occurred. This means that students should be able to complete homework assignments with high rates of success (Alleman, et al., 2010).

4. **Provide time in class to begin homework.** This enables students to practice their learning in a structured, supportive environment. You can also reduce frustration by providing immediate support.

5. **Use grading judicially.** Not every homework assignment needs to be graded. Again, the goal of homework is to practice learning. If the whole class does poorly on an assignment, this may be an indication that the skill or subject may not have been taught in ways that fully enabled learning to occur. In grading, always strive to catch students learning.

6. **Recognize normality.** Students learn at different rates and achieve at different levels. This is normal. Some students will be below average in their ability to learn certain school-related things. This is also normal and to be expected. Do not add to the feeling of abnormality students sometimes feel by (a) expecting uniformity in learning, (b) imposing unrealistic expectations on them, or (c) making comparisons to peers.

7. **Recognize growth and improvement.** Help students set appropriate learning goals. These goals should be different for each student. Contract grading is one way to do this (Johnson, 2017).

8. **Use strategies to reduce test anxiety.** One way to reduce test anxiety is to focus on learning instead of measuring learning. Just as a pig does not get heavier by weighing it, more learning does not occur with more testing. You could allow students to take more than one version of an exam. With today's technology, online exams can be created that randomly generate questions from a test bank. Each test will be slightly different. Allow students to study or even discuss results in small

groups between exams. Remember: The goal is learning—not measurement. And also teach test-taking strategies.

Negative Emotions Related to Learning Content

Negative emotions such as boredom, apathy, or frustration are sometimes linked with learning. This can occur when students are asked to learn things that they have no desire to learn or that have no connection to their lives. While not every learning experience in school can be new and exciting, not every learning experience needs to be dull or irrelevant. Providing places in the curriculum that offer choice can negate some of the negative emotions. Three types of choice are described here. As you review these, keep in mind that choice does not mean total choice all the time. There are very few learning situations where this would be appropriate. Instead, it is recommended that some choices be offered some of the time.

1. **Choice of content**. Here, students are able to make choices about what they learn. There are two types of content choices. The first is total choice. For example, Ms. Martinez has a box in the back of her fourth-grade classroom where students are able to put in lists of questions or topics of interest. She then uses her teacher expertise and creativity to design new lessons, insert topics within the current curriculum, or find books and other reading material related to students' questions or interests. The second type of content choice is giving students a choice among several different topics. Here a teacher identifies three to five content choices all related to the designated curriculum. Students are then able to make choices about which ones to study.
2. **Choice of content delivery.** Choice of content delivery reflects the types of choices offered in Universal Design for Learning (UDL) (Johnson, 2017). Here students are able to choose how the content is delivered. Delivery options could include things such as: (a) online mini-lectures created by the teacher, (b) small group instruction or activities, (c) independent learning programs, (d) graphic organizers to make content more visual, (e) lectures with guided notes, (f) Internet or video presentations, or (f) learning centers or stations.
3. **Choice of activity and assessment.** This also represents a type of choice offered in UDL. Students are able to select projects or activities to apply the information they have learned (Johnson, 2017). They are also able to make choices about how to demonstrate their learning. Examples here would be (a) giving small group speeches, (b) creating a graphic organizer, (c) preparing problem-based projects, (d) creating a short video presentation, or (e) taking mini-quizzes.

OPERANT CONDITIONING

Operant conditioning uses behavior modification strategies to reward behaviors that you wish to increase and punish behaviors that you wish to decrease. There are a variety of related strategies of varying levels of complexity that you can use in a classroom. Described here are two fairly simple yet effective such strategies: contingency contracts and token economies.

A Contingency Contract

A contingency contract is a form of behavior modification that is effective in focusing on one or two specific behaviors. Contingency contracts involve an "if/then" or "when/then" situation. Here, receiving a reward of some sort is contingent on a student's behavior. The contingency contract provides a visual record and external reminder for the student. It also provides immediate feedback and holds the student accountable for his or her behavior.

For example, Mr. Harris, a third-grade teacher, used a contingency contract with one of his students, Emma. Emma had trouble on the playground with other children; she got into fights and was not considerate of others. She also sometimes forgot classroom rules and acted out in class. At conference time Mr. Harris talked with Emma's parents and introduced the idea of a contingency contract. Mr. Harris identified two behaviors that he wanted to increase: (a) being considerate of others on the playground and (b) following classroom rules. With the approval of Emma's parents, Mr. Harris started using a contingency contract.

Mr. Harris broke the day into four sections: early morning, late morning, early afternoon, and later afternoon. Recess and lunch breaks were used to denote early and late mornings and afternoons. For each section of the day, Emma was given a rating: 2 = good job, 1= okay, and 0 = we need to try again. If Emma did an especially good job, Mr. Harris would give her a rating of 3. If Emma had a score of 20 or greater at the end of the week, she would be allowed to watch TV or play video games at home that night. If she had a score of 25 or greater, she would be able to select a movie to watch or do something special with her parents. (When using contingency contracts, it is best to start with low criteria to ensure early success, then raise the criteria gradually. This is also a form of shaping.)

This contract was taped inside of Emma's desk. Mr. Harris was able to give Emma fairly immediate feedback on her behavior four times a day. At the end of the week, Emma brought his contract to share with the principal or guidance counselor. This allowed Emma to get recognition for positive behavior or to explain where she needed to do better next time. After three weeks, Mr. Harris was able to give ratings just twice a day. After another two weeks he was able to give feedback just once a day, and eventually the contract was discontinued.

Token Economy

A token economy is a behavior modification system whereby students are able to earn a token such as a chip, a star, a check mark, or some sort of artificial money for outstanding performance related to academic performance, social skills, or friendship behaviors. Students are then able to use their tokens to buy some sort of reward or privilege such as eating lunch with the teacher, extra reading time, or prizes. Whereas contingency contracts are used with an individual student or a small number of students, token economies can be used as a classroom or schoolwide strategy.

At Grantsburg Elementary School, students were given a blue card every time a teacher caught them doing something positive (like helping a classmate), meeting a goal (either academic, behavioral, or personal), or doing an outstanding job at something. Teachers consciously rewarded different types of behaviors at different times. In this way it was similar to an intermittent reinforcement schedule. For example, one day Mr. Moore saw four of his second-grade students displaying a behavior that he wanted to see more often. He said, "I like the way this table came in and got ready for reading class without being asked. Nice job." He handed each of them a blue card right after he noticed the behavior (immediacy). Every two weeks the school would gather for an all-school meeting. As part of this meeting, all the blue cards were put in a bucket and there was a drawing for several different prizes. Instead of using punishment, this was a positive way to both teach and reinforce positive behaviors.

FOUR OTHER APPLICATIONS

Four other applications of behavioral learning theories are described here.

Immediacy

For reinforcement or punishment to be effective, it should occur immediately after the behavior. For example, to reinforce lever-pressing in a mouse, the food pellet needs to appear immediately upon pressing the lever. To reinforce hand-raising in children (instead of shouting out answers), some sort of reinforcement needs to be provided immediately after the behavior occurs such as saying, "I like the way Pat has her hand raised. Nice job, Pat. I can call on you." One thing to keep in mind with reinforcement and human beings is that what may be reinforcing to one may not be so to another. We are not standardized products. While some children crave attention and are reinforced by it, others do not. The key in using reinforcement effectively is to know your students and use what they naturally like to reinforce and shape the positive behaviors you would like to see.

In another example, Robert, in Mr. Jorgensen's fourth-grade class had been struggling with learning certain friendship behaviors. Mr. Jorgensen knows that when students are learning new behaviors, he needs to reinforce them anytime he sees semblances of them. This reinforcer can be fairly quiet and simple. For example, when he saw Robert remembering to use one of the friendship behaviors, he quietly said, "Robert, I really like how you remembered to listen and let people talk in your small group today. Nice job." This reinforcer could also be made public. For example, after seeing Robert work well in a cooperative group, Mr. Jorgensen said, "Robert, you really worked well with your cooperative learning group today. I am going to let your group have first choice of activities during free time today."

Natural Inclination (Premack Principle)

The Premack Principle states that more reliable behaviors can be used to reinforce less reliable behaviors. In other words, instead of looking for external rewards, identify what students like to do and use this as a reward. For example, in the upper elementary and middle school grades students enjoy talking with each other. A teacher might say, "If you stay focused on your homework for the next fifteen minutes, you can use the last five minutes to talk with your friends."

Law of Readiness

The law of readiness states that when an organism is ready to act, it is reinforcing for it to do so and annoying for it not to do so. When it is not ready to act, forcing it to do so is annoying. When a student is ready to learn, being able to do so is reinforcing. Not being able to do so is annoying. This suggests that motivation is an important aspect of learning and should be given much more consideration than is currently the case in most school settings. Motivation here refers, not to gaining rewards or avoiding punishment, but to the intrinsic desire to do something. Too little attention is given here. As described throughout this book, learning experiences are more powerful when they are based on students' intrinsic desire to learn and to find out about themselves and the world in which they live.

What are your students curious about? What do they want to learn? What concerns do they have in their lives? What would they like to be able to do? Why not ask them? This could be the start of some real learning. This does not mean that you need to abandon your curriculum or ignore the content standards that have been assigned to you. This instead is an invitation to adopt and adapt the curriculum to meet the needs and interests of your students. This, by the way, is what makes teaching exciting and interesting and keeps so many excellent teachers coming back every year. Teaching is a creative, intellectual endeavor when teachers are empowered to make choices regarding what and how to teach.

Behavioral Objectives

Behavioral learning theory defines learning as a change in behavior that occurs as a result of an experience. From this perspective learning should be behaviorally defined. In planning lessons, this takes the form of a behavioral objective. A behavioral objective is a single sentence that defines learning in terms of a behavior you would like to see as a result of instruction. You should be able to say yes or no to this question: Was that learning behavior observed? Examples of behavioral objectives include the following:

• Students will create a Venn diagram to illustrate similarities and differences between Hmong cultures and their own culture.
• Students will demonstrate their knowledge of asteroids by completing the post-lesson worksheet with a score of 95 percent or higher.
• Students will demonstrate their knowledge of amphibians by successfully completing the amphibian worksheet.
• Students will identify and describe the essential elements of classical conditioning.
• Students will be able to correctly identify the verbs used in their daily writing sample.

By describing lesson plan objectives in terms of particular behaviors that you want students to demonstrate, you are able to focus your planning and instruction to make those behaviors appear. In the lesson plan, everything that follows should support the objective. If an activity does not support the objective, do not include it. More about learning objectives will be described in chapter 20.

Chapter Seven

Social Cognitive Learning Theory

This chapter is an appropriate place to begin transitioning from behavioral learning theories to cognitive learning theories. Originally social cognitive learning theory was called simply "social learning theory." It was considered a behavioral learning theory because it involved observing the behaviors of others and the resulting rewards and punishments. Future behaviors were then based on these observations. However, social learning theory eventually incorporated many ideas from cognitive learning theory (Ormrod, 2012), hence the current name, social cognitive theory. (Note: Although the name of this theory is social cognitive learning theory, the term *social learning* will be used here to denote the learning that occurs.)

THE BASICS

From the perspective of *social cognitive learning theory*, learning is a change in mental processes that creates the capacity to demonstrate different behaviors that occur as a result of observing others.

For example:

Mary watches Sam. Mary sees Sam get punished for a behavior. Mary avoids that behavior.

Mary watches Pat. Mary sees Pat get rewarded for a behavior. Mary demonstrates that behavior.

Mary watches Francis do it. Mary sees how it is done. Mary does it.

Cognition plays a part in social learning in the form of expectations. After observing a model and noting the resulting rewards or punishments, it is expected that if one behaves in a similar way, one will get rewarded or punished similarly. Instead of having to go through trial-and-error learning (*incremental learning*), where the incorrect responses are gradually eliminat-ed, people are able to benefit immediately from observing the success or failure of others (*insightful learning*).

Social learning is a form of *vicarious learning* in that it occurs by observ-ing others. *Enactive learning* is when learning occurs by doing. Students learn best when both are combined. That is, when they observe others and are then able to practice what was observed. This is true of both social and academic skills.

Four Conditions Necessary for Social Learning

There are four conditions necessary for social learning to take place:

1. **Attention.** Learners need to attend to the behavior to be learned. In a classroom, teachers sometimes have to point out specific behaviors. "Boys and girls, did you notice how . . ." Also, teachers sometimes have to ask students to look for specific behaviors. "When you go into the lunchroom today, I want you to notice how the sixth-grade class . . ." A wrestling coach might call attention to salient elements of a move before the demonstration. "When Rory does the single leg takedown, notice how he . . ." Or a teacher might say, "When I [insert skill], notice how [insert salient element]." These are all examples of calling attention to what students should learn.

2. **Retention.** The observer must be able to remember what was ob-served later when given opportunities to act. Posters with reminders, concept maps, and graphic organizers are all ways to call attention to salient elements. Verbal reminders also can be used. "We're going to the library. Let's remember the three important things we learned about . . ." Or, "When doing long division, remember to . . ."

3. **Production.** Observers must be given opportunities to reproduce or practice the behavior. However, observers must also be able to repro-duce the behavior. That is, the behavior must be proximal. A teacher could have an expert tap dancer come into a third-grade classroom and model dancing; but if most students are not able to reproduce the behavior, it would be an ineffective social learning situation.

4. **Motivation.** The observer must be motivated to act. That means that the observer must value the behavior or the rewards that come as a result of the behavior. In addition, the observer must expect to see some sort of reinforcement occur as a result of the behavior.

ALBERT BANDURA AND THE BOBO DOLL

One of the classic studies in psychology related to social learning was conducted by Albert Bandura and colleagues (Bandura, Ross and Ross, 1961). Here, children were shown a film where adults interacted aggressively (hitting, punching, and kicking) with an inflatable toy known as a Bobo doll. Children were put into four different groups:

- **Group 1: rewards.** Children watched a film version where the adult was rewarded for the aggressive behavior.
- **Group 2: punishment.** Children watched a film version where the adult was punished for the aggressive behavior.
- **Group 3: no consequences**. Children watched a film version where there were no consequences for the adult's aggressive behavior.
- **Group 4: control.** This was the control group. Children were not shown any films.

After watching the film, children were put in a room in which there was a Bobo doll. The children who saw the adult rewarded for aggressive behavior (Group 1) were more likely to behave aggressively when compared to the other groups. Children who saw the adult punished for aggressive behavior (Group 2) were less likely to behave aggressively when compared to the other groups. This study suggested that children's future behaviors are strongly influenced by observing the behavior of adults and how they are rewarded and punished.

MODELING

Social learning includes behavioral, cognitive, and affective changes that occur as a result of observing models. There are three types of modeling. The first, *direct modeling*, is where one attempts to directly imitate another's behavior. For example, Sam observed Mary studying and noticed how she studied. He saw that she got A's on most of her exams. Sam wanted to be as successful as Mary. He began to study in the same way that Mary did.

The second, *symbolic modeling*, is where one imitates the behaviors of characters in movies, in books, in video games, or on television. This occurs frequently with teenagers and the various media they consume. For example, Phil began talking and dressing the way characters do on his favorite TV show.

The third, *synthesized modeling*, is where one takes bits and pieces from a variety of models. For example, Harvey was a beginning teacher. He took ideas and modeled his teaching style from a variety of teachers that he observed during student teaching and his first year of teaching.

A model's influence is determined by the following factors (Gerrig and Zimbardo, 2008):

- **Status of the model.** The model is perceived positively, liked, and respected. Models with high prestige and who are older or more powerful are more apt to influence observational learning.
- **Similarity of the model.** There are perceived similarities between the model and the observer.
- **Potential for modeling.** The model's behavior is within the observer's range of competence to imitate the behavior. That is, they have the capacity to imitate the task.
- **Perceived competence of the model.** The model is perceived as competent.
- **Reinforcing consequences.** The model gets rewarded or punished for the behavior.
- **Noticeable behavior.** The model's behavior stands out against the background of competing models.

IMPLICATIONS

Social learning can be used to help students develop positive behaviors and enhance teaching and learning.

Helping Students Develop Positive Behaviors

Here are four ideas for using social learning to develop positive behaviors:

1. **Good books.** Have an abundance of high-quality books available that include characters with positive character traits. In this book collection make sure there is an equal number of male and female lead characters who are similar in age (or a little older) to the students who are reading them. These books should enable students to see the logical consequences of both positive and negative behavior without having to experience the circumstances themselves. However, books should not involve moralizing or propaganda, as this often has the opposite intended effect.
2. **Model.** Model the behaviors you wish to see. Keep in mind that your interactions with students and colleagues are always being watched. If your interactions demonstrate respect for those with whom you interact, these attitudes are more likely to be reflected by your students. Children learn what they live.

3. **Moral dilemmas.** Include moral dilemmas within the classroom or curriculum. *Moral dilemmas* are descriptions of real-life situations in which a decision needs to be made that does not have a clear-cut answer. Students are put into small groups and asked to come to a consensus on the decision. Children develop the capacity for moral reasoning and advance more quickly to higher levels by practicing their reasoning skills and hearing the moral reasoning of others (Johnson, 2009).
4. **Cognitive modeling.** *Cognitive modeling* is thinking aloud to demonstrate a cognitive process. Here you make your thinking visible. Use this to let students hear you think as you reason through a social problem or a dilemma involving values.

Using Social Learning Theory to Enhance Teaching and Learning

Social learning also can be used to enhance the teaching and learning of academic subjects and skills. Five ideas are presented here:

1. **Student demonstrations.** Look for students who do a particular skill well. Allow them to demonstrate to others or teach in small groups.
2. **Social interaction.** Create learning experiences that utilize social interaction. This could include structured conversations, cooperative learning assignments, or problem-solving activities related to curriculum content in which students are able to work together and hear the thinking and reasoning of others.
3. **Multiage classrooms**. Multiage classrooms contain two or three grade levels within a single class. This creates a variety of opportunities for many forms of social learning to occur.
4. **Cognitive modeling**. *Cognitive modeling* also can be used to teach complex skills or cognitive processes.
5. **Elements of effective skills instruction.** In teaching academic skills, use the elements of effective skills instruction (Johnson, 2017). These lessons consist of input, guided practice, and independent practice. Here teacher modeling is included in the input part of the lesson. Students are then able to practice what was modeled in the guided practice and independent practice parts of the lesson (see chapter 9).

Part IV

Cognitive Learning Theories

Chapters 8 to 15 examine cognitive learning theories. These theories share a common view of learning. From this perspective, learning is a change in cognitive structures that occurs as a result of instruction or experience. These next chapters will examine several cognitive learning theories. You will notice that neurological learning theory has many elements in common with these theories. Neurological learning theory often describes and confirms elements of cognitive learning theory from a physiological perspective.

- Chapter 8: Piaget's Learning Theory
- Chapter 9: Vygotsky's Learning Theory
- Chapter 10: The Information Processing Model
- Chapter 11: Memory
- Chapter 12: Learning
- Chapter 13: Constructivist Learning Theory
- Chapter 14: The Learning Theory of Jerome Bruner
- Chapter 15: Ausubel's Theory of Meaningful Verbal Learning

Chapter Eight

Piaget's Learning Theory

This chapter examines the learning theory of Jean Piaget (1896–1980), a biologist who studied zoology and earned his PhD in natural sciences in 1918. He went on to study psychology and children's cognitive development. His theories related to intelligence and learning very much reflect his background as a biologist.

LEARNING

Whereas behavioral learning theories describe learning in terms of observable behaviors, cognitive learning theories describe learning in terms of the mind and the acquisition and organization of knowledge. *Learning* here is a change in cognitive structures that occurs as a result of instruction or experience.

Some Basic Terms

- **Cognitive structure** is the name given for the organized body of knowledge in our head. In neurological terms, this would be the series of neural networks that make up the cortex. A file cabinet is a useful metaphor here. Within this file cabinet are the individual file folders related to specific bodies of information called *schema* or *schemata* (plural). A schema would be a neural network related to specific knowledge. Schemata are used to make sense of new information. As we learn more, our schemata become more organized and complex. In turn, our thinking becomes more sophisticated. Since we use our existing schemata to interpret new information, the larger our schematic filing system (our knowledge base) the more we are able to learn.

- **Adaptation,** according to Piaget's theory, is the process through which learning occurs. It is the natural tendency to adjust to one's environment using *assimilation* and *accommodation*.
- **Assimilation** occurs when we encounter new information that corresponds with our existing schemata or fits within our cognitive framework. For example, in his second-grade science class, Bobby learns that frogs hibernate during the winter. This new information fits within his current frog schema. Assimilation occurs as this new information is used to expand this existing schema.
- **Accommodation** occurs when we encounter new information that either does not fit within our schemata or where no schema exists related to this new information. For example, as Bobby gets older, he learns that animals today look much different than they did a million years ago. He encounters the theory of evolution for the first time. This conflicts with his current schemata. Accommodation occurs when Bobby restructures his schemata to incorporate this new information. In this case Bobby had to rethink some of his basic understandings.

     Learning requires both assimilation and accommodation. Assimilation because new information is based on old information. Accommodation because new information requires existing schemata to be reorganized or new schemata to be created.
- **Equilibration** is the motivating force behind all learning. It is a natural desire to make sense of the world, to create meaning out of confusion, or to move from disequilibrium back to equilibrium (see the next section).

A Theory of Learning

Piaget's learning theory was devised originally to describe the learning process of children, but the same learning process applies to learners of all ages and levels. This is how it works: We start out in a state of equilibrium where things make sense. When new information or novel phenomena are encountered that do not correspond with our existing knowledge, a state of disbalance or disequilibrium is created. This is a very dissatisfying mental state. Humans naturally seek to create new understandings. We move from disequilibrium to equilibrium using both assimilation and accommodation. Once equilibration has been achieved, new interests and phenomena again move us to a state of disequilibrium, and the cycle of learning continues. It is the natural desire to achieve equilibrium that promotes the development of new knowledge as well as more complex levels of knowledge.

Applications

Like a scientist doing experiments and conducting research, children try to make sense of their environment through play or just messing around. The following applications of this theory are appropriate for learners at all levels.

First, create pre-reading or pre-lesson activities that lead to a state of disequilibrium. To do this, (a) pique learners' natural curiosity by posing a question, (b) provide a unique experience that does not quite make sense, or (c) present an overview that leaves out something that only can be understood or discovered by reading the story or chapter or by attending to the lesson.

Second, design learning experiences that allow for experimenting and messing around. Discovery learning, inquiry learning, problem-based learning, and experiential learning are pedagogical strategies that allow for this in varying degrees (Johnson, 2017).

PIAGET'S STAGES OF COGNITIVE DEVELOPMENT

The focus of this book is on learning theories (as opposed to cognitive development). As such, just the basics of Piaget's theory related to cognitive development are described here.

Before Piaget, people thought children's brains functioned much the same as adults. It was assumed that they just needed to be filled with raw knowledge and experiences in order to function in an adult manner. However, Piaget observed that our brains and mental functioning develop through a series of universal stages and that we think in distinctly different ways at each stage.

Stages

According to Piaget, changes in thinking are a result of developmental processes that occur naturally as our brains develop. All children, he said, go through four stages:

- **Sensorimotor stage** (birth to approximately age two). Children's early cognitive development is largely controlled by their senses and their ability to move, hence the label *sensorimotor*. Thinking here is largely representational. *Representational thinking* is the ability to picture (or represent) something in one's mind.
- **Preoperational stage** (approximately age two to seven). Piaget described an *operation* as an action carried out through logical thinking. Having acquired representational thinking, preoperational thinking is the stage just before children are able to use formalized logic. Here vocabularies

expand from two hundred to around two thousand or more words. Although children are learning language and language rules, they do not yet understand logical relationships and cannot mentally manipulate information. This stage is marked by *irreversible thinking*, the ability to think in only one direction (they cannot reverse an operation). For example, they may know that 2+1 = 3, but they cannot use reverse logic to understand that 3-2 = 1. Preoperational children are also highly *egocentric* in that they have a hard time taking another person's point of view. They still see the world only in terms of themselves.

- **Concrete operational stage** (approximately age seven to eleven). This stage is marked by the beginning of logical thinking. For example, irreversible thinking begins to give way to reversible thinking. That is, children are now able to understand that that 3-2 = 1 is the reverse of 2+1 = 3. However, all thinking is very concrete and based in the present. Thus, when introducing numbers and the concepts of addition and subtraction, children in preschool through grade one should be given chips, buttons, or other concrete counters to see and manipulate. Likewise, all science instruction should be as hands-on and active as possible (learning by doing vs. learning by listening, watching, or reading).

- **Formal operational** (approximately age eleven on). At this stage children begin to acquire the ability to think abstractly. That is, they are just beginning to be able to develop and manipulate symbols and generalize concepts to similar situations. For example, they are able to make the following mental operations: If A is greater than B and B is greater than C, then A is greater than C. Or, make analogies such as Big is to little as slow is to (a) wide, (b) turtle, or (c) fast. Or even create abstract metaphors such as: Math class was a big puddle of mud. And, given a set of facts, they are able to make inferences.

Application

The application here is that instruction and educational experiences must be developmentally appropriate. Hence the term *developmentally appropriate practice*. If children are not developmentally ready, certain types of instruction or experiences will be ineffective or sometimes even detrimental. For example, the type of reading "instruction" given to children at the preoperational stage should look much different from the type given to children at the concrete operational and formal operational stages (Johnson, 2016). Putting sounds to symbols and putting symbols together to form words is a fairly abstract endeavor. Instead, reading "instruction" at this stage should involve exposure to lots of good books. Instruction related to letter sounds should be very brief and set in the context of these books. It is not developmentally appropriate to begin formalized phonics instruction using worksheets at this level.

Developmentally appropriate practice is instruction that fits students' social, emotional, cognitive, and physical developmental levels. Students will be interested and ready to learn topics and skills when (a) they are developmentally ready, (b) they are able to learn in developmentally appropriate ways, and (c) instruction and topics are attuned to their natural desires and inclinations.

Chapter Nine

Vygotsky's Learning Theory

Lev Vygotsky (1896–1924) was a psychiatry and psychology researcher. According to Lev Vygotsky's sociocultural theory, thinking develops from the outside in. As children interact with others and hear words around them, and as they observe the interactions of others, they *internalize* language patterns (Vygotsky, 1978). These language patterns gradually evolve into thought patterns or ways of thinking. The same thing happens as children are immersed in a particular culture with its vast array of symbols, values, and ways of viewing reality. Through this type of immersion, they gradually take on the thought patterns of their culture. Thus, children's social and cultural interactions shape and help develop their thinking and their view of the world (hence, the name *sociocultural theory*). Vygotsky's theory posits that thinking begins on a social level and is then internalized.

DEVELOPING HIGHER MENTAL FUNCTIONS

According to Vygotsky, humans start out life with a set of *lower mental functions* that are genetically inherited. These involve things such as reflexes, attention, and perception. These functions are controlled in large part by the environment. That is, cognition is generally limited to a human's response and reaction to environmental stimuli. As children hear language around them, and as they interact with other humans and their culture, these lower functions develop and eventually evolve into higher functions.

Lower mental functions involve those in which there is no processing of incoming stimuli. This include reflexes (sucking, grasping), attention, awareness, rudimentary conscious processes, association, elementary perception, and visual memory. *Higher mental functions* are those cognitive operations that involve the processing of incoming stimuli. These include voluntary

63

attention, willful memory, logical memory, planning, decision-making, reasoning, problem-solving, and semantic memory. It is by being exposed to social interaction, language, and culture that these mental functions move from lower to higher levels.

ZONE OF PROXIMAL DEVELOPMENT AND SCAFFOLDING

The application of this learning theory is described here in the context of learning a skill, but it can be applied to learning concepts as well. When learning a skill there are three levels of task difficulty. The *independent level* is the level at which students can perform a task by themselves without any help. The *instructional level* is the level at which students can perform a task with teacher support (or scaffolding). Another term for this is the *zone of proximal development* (ZPD). This is just above the instructional level but below the frustration level. The *frustration level* is the level at which, even with strong teacher support, students are not able to complete a task. To ask them to do so results in frustration (hence the name).

Scaffolding in an educational context is a strategy where the teacher provides some sort of structure or support so students can complete a task that is a little above their independent level. Scaffolding and the zone of proximal development are important concepts for success in any sort of teaching, whether it is in music, athletics, drama, forensics, business, math, or any other curriculum area. Here, a teacher would first find students' independent level and then get a little above with enough supports or scaffolding to enable them to succeed.

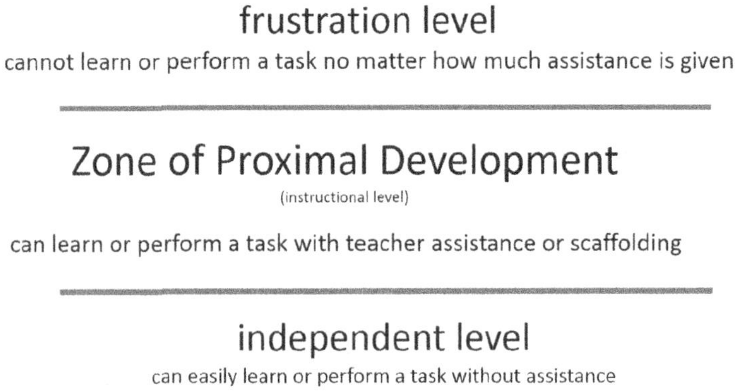

frustration level
cannot learn or perform a task no matter how much assistance is given

Zone of Proximal Development
(instructional level)

can learn or perform a task with teacher assistance or scaffolding

independent level
can easily learn or perform a task without assistance

Figure 9.1. Zone of proximal development.

For example, Ms. Lee was teaching double-digit addition to her second-grade math class. After briefly providing an overview, she used an example to demonstrate the steps. Then she handed out sheets of blank thinking paper to her students. As she provided a second example, she asked students to use their thinking paper to work along with her as she went through each step of the process. The students wrote on their paper exactly what Ms. Less wrote on the board. This is an example of scaffolding or guided instruction. She then provided a third example, except that this time she stopped and had students complete the last step independently. She was able to quickly walk around the room to check if students were on track. For the next example she left out an additional step. With each succeeding example, Ms. Lee left out an additional step. This is called a *gradual release of responsibility*. Here students are increasingly asked to do more of the steps of a skill independently during a guided period of instruction. This could be done independently or with a partner. Eventually, Ms. Lee's students were asked to do problems independently. She again walked around the room as students were working to see if they were on track. Ms. Lee then assigned four additional problems as homework so that students could practice what they just learned.

APPLICATION: A BASIC SKILLS LESSON PLAN

Effective skills instruction utilizing Vygotsky's learning theory includes four elements: (1) purpose statement, (2) direct instruction and modeling, (3) guided practice, and (4) independent practice. (Johnson, 2017). Each of these components is described here in the context of a skills lesson plan (see chapter 20).

1. **Purpose statement.** This is a one-sentence statement that identifies the skill that you want students to learn about or be able to do.
2. **Input.** The input for teaching a skill is used to tell students exactly what they need to know in order to perform the skill. Here, you provide explicit instruction related to how the skill might be used and the specific steps. You also demonstrate and model the skill by thinking aloud while going through each step.
3. **Guided practice.** Sometimes referred to as scaffolded instruction, guided practice is at the heart of teaching a skill of any kind (Johnson, 2000). The goal here is to provide the support necessary for students to use the skill independently. This is where you take the whole class through each step of the skill several times, providing a gradual release of responsibility.
4. **Independent practice.** This is an activity designed to enable students to independently practice or reinforce the skill they have just learned.

This may include an in-class activity or homework. If the skills lesson has been taught effectively, students should be able to complete this with 95 to 100 percent success ratio (Alleman, et al., 2010).

Regular practice, review, and integration is not part of the skills lesson plan; however, it should be understood that mastery of any skill never occurs with a single lesson or exposure. With any skill, students need to revisit and review it many times for it to become part of their cognitive repertoire. Regular practice allows for efficiency and automaticity.

APPLICATION: COGNITIVE APPRENTICESHIPS AND MODELING

To utilize the social nature of learning, teachers sometimes pair novice students with expert students in particular areas. This usually occurs in problem-solving or critical-thinking activities in which the novice is able to hear the thinking or reasoning process of the expert. The term for this is *cognitive apprenticeship*. This can occur when an older learner is paired with a younger learner, such as multilevel or multigraded classrooms. This also can occur when teachers work through problems with students using *cognitive modeling*. This is when teachers think aloud in order to model their thinking process.

Chapter Ten

The Information-Processing Model

Cognitive learning theories describe learning in terms of the mind and acquisition and organization of knowledge. The information-processing model examined in this chapter helps in understanding this process.

HOW THE MODEL WORKS

We will begin by defining our terms: Your *brain* is the physical organ responsible for your learning and thinking. *Mind* is the term for the psychological phenomena that the brain enables. *Consciousness* is the product of the mind or that of which you are aware. The *information-processing model* (sometimes called the *standard memory model*) describes how the mind inputs, analyzes, organizes, stores, and retrieves information (Johnson, 2013). This process involves three types of memory: sense memory, short-term memory, and long-term memory (see figure 10.1).

Sense Memory

At any given moment we encounter sense data in the form of sights, sounds, smells, feelings, and tastes. These are called *stimuli*. *Perception* is the detection of stimuli through one of our five senses. We are bombarded with millions of stimuli every day. However, if we were to attend to all the stimuli we encountered we would be overwhelmed. Thus we make decisions about which stimuli get our attention.

Attention involves the choices we make about which perceived stimuli to allow into our consciousness in order to assign meaning. You decide which particular stimulus upon which to focus or attend. For example, as you are reading this text you are choosing to attend to the visual stimuli in front of

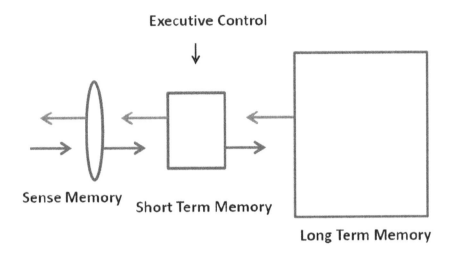

Executive Control

Sense Memory   **Short Term Memory**

Long Term Memory

Figure 10.1.   Information-processing model.

you in the form of letters and words. You are most likely ignoring the sounds in the background, the sound of your own breath, or the feel of the clothes against your skin. You are making choices about blocking some stimuli while allowing others to move into your consciousness. If you did not make these choices, comprehending the words and ideas in front of you would be very difficult.

Sense memory, sometimes called *sensory register*, is where this original sense data is perceived. It has an unlimited capacity; however, it has a very short duration. It retains an exact copy of what is perceived, but this only lasts for one to three seconds.

Short-Term Memory

While the terms *short-term memory* and *working memory* are often used synonymously, technically they are different. Shortterm memory (STM) is like a small holding pen for perceived data from sense memory. It also can hold information recalled from long-term memory (more on this later). STM has a limited capacity. It can hold seven plus or minus two (7+/-2) bits of information. This means that most people can hold seven bits of information; however, some can hold up to nine bits and some only five bits. This is not a lot of information.

Holding bits longer. The duration of STM is about fifteen seconds. After this, things begin to fade. There are two ways to hold onto things longer: The first is called *maintenance rehearsal*. This is repeating things many times.

For example, Sally met Bill. Bill gave Sally his phone number. She had nothing to write with, so she repeated the number many times so that it would sticks in her long-term memory (LTM). This is an example of maintenance rehearsal.

The other trick is called *elaborative rehearsal.* Here you associate what is to be remembered with something meaningful. For example, the combination to Pat's gym locker combination was 30-20-14. To hold on to these numbers in STM and eventually commit them to (LTM), Pat associated each with an age. He elaborated by picturing himself at age thirty, twenty, and fourteen. This made it easier to hold these random numbers in the STM and to retrieve them from LTM when he needed them.

Holding more bits. *Chunking* can be used to hold more information in STM. This is when you organize bits of data into meaningful larger wholes. This enables you to make more efficient use of the limited space in STM and to hold more information.

To illustrate, let us imagine you were given ten seconds to memorize the following sixteen digits: 1-9-7-2-2-0-1-0-1-9-9-8-1-7-7-6. You would probably be able to remember five to seven of them. If instead we chunked them into more meaningful wholes (double digits) and asked you to memorize them (19-72–20–10-19-98-17-76), you would be probably able to remember five to seven of these double digit numbers for a total of twelve to fourteen total digits. Finally, if we chunked them into larger units (1972-2010-1998-1776), you would most likely be able to remember all four of these larger units for a total of sixteen digits. In this last condition, the numbers were chunked into meaningful wholes related to years. The digits were the same in each case and presented in the same order. The difference was only in how they were grouped. This is chunking.

Working memory. Whereas STM is a passive receptacle, *working memory* is an active space within STM used to work with information. This is where you add to data, analyze data, organize data, restructure data, or make connections.

Working memory is also the place where *metacognition* takes place. Metacognition means thinking about thinking. Here you monitor your own thoughts or check for understanding. This is often used to describe what happens during reading when you ask yourself, "Do I understanding what I'm reading? Does this make sense? Do I need to read this paragraph again?" Metacognition is also used in the act of listening or learning. During a lecture you would ask questions such as, "What's the main point here? How is this like something else I've learned? Does this make sense?"

Automaticity. *Automaticity* is the act of performing a procedure or cognitive operation without thinking about it or with very little conscious awareness. In other words, the thinking processes involved with a procedure are automatic. The best example of this is driving a car. As we drive, most of us do not have to consciously think about pressing the gas pedal or the brake pedal or turning the wheel. We respond to the curves and stop signs we encounter automatically with very little conscious attention. Automaticity frees up space in STM allowing us to devote more attention to other things such as road conditions or other cars.

Developing automaticity with any skill enables us to devote more space in STM to high-level thinking. The skill most associated with automaticity in school is reading. Here we want children to develop automaticity in recognizing words. In this way they are better able to analyze and evaluate ideas and engage in high-level thinking as they read. Automaticity is important in other skill areas as well, including writing, mathematics, and keyboarding.

Long-Term Memory

LTM has an almost unlimited capacity to store information for an almost unlimited duration. This means that everything we have ever experienced is tucked away in our brains somewhere. Why then do we forget? It is not a matter of storage; rather, it's a matter of retrieval. That is, the information is still in our memory; we just have a hard time getting access to some of it.

The storage locker analogy. Putting data in and taking it out of LTM is very much like putting things in a rented storage locker. Three important terms in this process are *encoding, storage,* and *retrieval. Encoding* is the process of organizing and putting data into LTM. This is like gathering up your things, sorting them, putting them into boxes and plastic storage bins with labels, and putting them into the storage locker in an organized fashion. *Storage* is the actual holding of information in LTM. This is like a storage locker filled with boxes and bins. *Retrieval* is getting access to information found LTM and pulling it back out into STM. This is like going into the storage locker, getting specific things from the boxes or bins, and taking them out so that you can use them. If the things in the storage locker are organized, with related things next to each other, it is much easier to find and retrieve exactly what you need.

Our brains naturally organize new information. However, we will see in the chapters that follow that there are things that you can do to enhance students' ability to encode, store, and retrieve information.

Learning and memory. Learning is different from remembering. Remembering is simply being able to recall or retrieve information from LTM. Remembering does not involve understanding. Learning is the ability to use the information, connect new information to current knowledge, or create meaning with the information. (Memory will be examined in more depth in the next chapter.)

THE TWO-WAY FLOW OF INFORMATION

Information does not simply flow from sense memory to STM and up to LTM. In the act of perception, encoding, and retrieval, it also flows down from LTM to STM to sense memory. This replicates what was described in earlier chapters related to neurological learning theory.

From LTM to STM

Information in LTM moves into STM to help us understand and encode information. And, the more knowledge about a particular topic we have in LTM, the easier it is to understand and encode information in STM (you will see this idea repeated in many places in this book).

For example, Professor Abrams knows a lot about educational psychology. When he encounters new information related to this topic, he is able to understand and encode it quickly and efficiently without much memory loss. It is not necessarily because his brain functions any better than yours does. It is because his LTM is full of educational psychology knowledge. This enables him to encode, store, and retrieve educational psychology information fairly easily. He knows exactly what to look for, where to store it, and how it relates to or is connected with other things.

However, when this same brain is exposed to information about dendrology, encoding seems to be slow, inefficient, and labored with much memory loss and very little understanding. This is because there is very little information in Professor Abrams's LTM related to this subject. The same brain is interacting with both the educational psychology information and the dendrology information, yet meaning and understanding vary greatly. What is different is the type and amount of knowledge in LTM.

LTM to Sense Memory and Perception

We also use information in LTM to help us perceive and attend to stimuli in sensory memory. Here are two specific examples of how LTM enhances perception. The first example occurs during the process of reading. As discussed briefly already, the knowledge in Professor Abrams's head related to educational psychology helps him to easily perceive and identify important words and concepts as he is reading. He is able to perceive the important words faster than he would words related to dendrology. Again, it is the knowledge in LTM that enhances this process.

The second example occurs when Professor Brown visits her students in an elementary classroom. Upon entering the room, she is able to quickly perceive a wide variety of data. This is because she taught in elementary classrooms for many years and has visited hundreds of classrooms as part of field experiences related to teacher-preparation programs. These experiences, combined with the related books and articles she has read and written, give her a very large storage bin in LTM related to these things. As such, she can go into a classroom and very quickly perceive things that her beginning students cannot. She can provide you with a sense of the overall emotional tone of the classroom, the effectiveness of instruction, the probable philosophy of the teacher, and the particular strengths of that teacher. In other words, she is able to perceive and quickly connect the data dots.

EXECUTIVE CONTROL

The last thing we will look at in this chapter is the executive control function of the information processing model. This is the mind behind the brain. This is also an area where educational psychology and educational philosophy overlap a bit. The human entity is not simply a brain responding to stimuli. Instead, there is a mind directing the brain. If we thought of the brain as a tractor, the mind would be the tractor driver who controls where attention is placed, what stimuli to attend to, what strategies to use, what information to encode and retrieve, what signals to send to various parts of the body, metacognition, and all other functioning. Right now your tractor driver is controlling where you put your attention as you look to create meaning with the words appearing in front of you.

Chapter Eleven

Memory

Learning involves both memory and knowledge. This chapter examines memory.

CONSTRUCTING MEMORIES

As described in previous chapters, human memory is constructed using what we know and believe along with context, expectations, and past experiences (Sternberg and Williams, 2009). Our memories never exactly replicate reality. Instead our memories are reconstructed versions of reality using all the information and experiences stored in long-term memory (LTM) (Revlin, 2013).

Types of Memory

There are three types of memories. *Semantic memory* is memory of concepts and ideas that are not of personal experience. This type of memory is important for school-related learning. *Episodic memory* is memory of events and experiences from our lives (episodes). Because of the emotional content, episodic memories are especially susceptible to memory reconstruction. *Procedural memory*, often called "how to" memory is the ability to recall procedures, skills, or how to do things (procedural knowledge). Data related to each of these three types of memory are all stored differently in LTM. How we encode and retrieve one type of memory is different from how we encode and retrieve the other types of memories. Learning is enhanced when all three types of memory are used in the learning process.

Levels of Memory: Explicit and Implicit

There are two levels of memory. *Explicit memory* is the knowledge that can be recalled and consciously considered. This most often refers to semantic and episodic memories where you are able to bring knowledge or events to conscious awareness upon demand. Example: What did you have for breakfast today (episodic)? What is the state capital of Wisconsin (semantic)? However, procedural memory can also be explicit. Examples: What are the steps used in long division? How do I use the skills lesson plan format?

Implicit memory includes those memories that are out of awareness but can still influence our thoughts or behaviors. These are sometimes called unconscious memories (memories of which we are not conscious, but which can be brought into awareness under the right circumstances) or subconscious memories (memories below our consciousness awareness that we are not able to access). There are three types of implicit memories: procedural, conditioned, and primed (Woolfolk, 2007). *Implicit procedural memories* involve those skills that have become automatic (automaticity). For example, you know how to drive a car or ride a bike automatically. You do not have to think about it. Implicit procedural memories also include habits you may have formed (you make coffee first thing in the morning without thinking about it) or ways of doing things (you always put on your right sock and shoe and then the left sock and shoe).

The second type of implicit memories, *implicit conditioned memories*, is related to classical conditioning. Here you unconsciously associate episodic memories to current environmental stimuli. For example, you become anxious when you are asked to bat in a baseball game because you remember getting hit in the head by a pitch in seventh grade. Or you respond positively to a commercial with a dog in it because of your own pleasurable dog experiences.

The third type of implicit memories involves priming or activating related information in LTM. *Primed implicit memories* are those that are directly related or closely related to something else you are retrieving. For example, in an education class studying lesson planning your instructor uses a social studies lesson plan as an example. You suddenly remember a particular social studies class you had in middle school. The example triggers something with which it was paired in LTM. A similar thing triggered an associated memory. This is an example of a primed implicit memory.

Knowledge and Memory

Knowledge is highly correlated with memory. In a classic experiment, chess experts and novices were asked to memorize the positions of chess pieces on a board for five seconds (Chase and Simon, 1973). The experts were significantly better at being able to remember and reconstruct the positions of the pieces when the pieces involved real-life configurations (those that imitated a real-life chess game). However, when the pieces were placed randomly on the board, there were no differences between novices and experts. This suggests that our memories are highly influenced by knowledge. As is described elsewhere in this book, knowledge is an important element of expertise in any area. This reinforces the importance of helping students develop a well-organized body of knowledge.

Retrieval Failure

Retrieval failure is another name for forgetting. Retrieval failure is information stored in LTM that cannot be accessed. Since memory does not decay unless brain cells are destroyed, things sometimes interfere or get in the way. *Interference* is the term used for retrieval impediments. *Retroactive interference* is retrieval failure caused by something that occurs after the initial learning. For example, Bill played tennis when he was growing up. He spent many years as an adult playing racquetball. One day he decided to play tennis after many years of playing racquetball; however, he found that he had a hard time remembering exactly how to swing the racquet and how to position himself on the court.

Proactive interference is retrieval failure caused by something that occurred before the initial learning or encoding. One semester Professor Samuels had a student in her classed named Beth Satterson. The only other time Professor Samuels had encountered someone with this last name was during her childhood. She had a classmate named Becky Satterson. Throughout the semester when Professor Samuels called on Beth, she kept calling her Becky, not Beth. Her previous learning was getting in the way of her current memories.

LEVELS-OF-PROCESSING THEORY

Retrieval failure also can be related to how information was initially encoded. According to the *levels-of-processing theory*, the more extensively we manipulate information during the encoding process, the easier it can be retrieved (Craik and Lockhart, 1972). In other words, students learn more deeply and are better able to retrieve and use information from LTM if they are actively engaged with the learning material during the learning process instead of simply being passive receivers of information. Active engagement avoids the problem of *inert knowledge*. This is where knowledge exists in LTM but cannot be retrieved or used.

Use Bloom's Taxonomy

In *Taxonomy of Educational Objectives* (1956), Benjamin Bloom described six levels of thinking. These six levels of thinking and the cognitive operations for each level can be used to design questions, activities, and assignments that actively engage students during and after lessons. Levels 1 and 2 have fairly low levels of cognitive engagement. Levels 3 and above generally have higher levels of cognitive engagement.

1. **Knowledge.** Recalls facts or remembers previously learned material. Knowledge-level operations include the following: define, describe, identify, list, match, name, tell, describe, show, label, collect, examine, tabulate, quote, duplicate, memorize, recognize, relate, recall, repeat, reproduce, or state.
2. **Comprehension.** Grasp the meaning of material. Comprehension-level operations include the following: interpret, explain, summarize, convert, defend, distinguish, estimate, generalize, rewrite, contrast, predict, associate, distinguish, estimate, differentiate, discuss, extend, classify, discuss, express, indicate, locate, recognize, report, restate, review, select, or translate.
3. **Application.** Use learned material in a new situation. Application-level operations include the following: apply, change, compute, demonstrate, operate, show, use, solve, calculate, complete, illustrate, examine, modify, relate, change, experiment, dramatize, employ, illustrate, interpret, operate, practice, schedule, sketch, or write.
4. **Analysis.** Break things down into parts in order to understand, organize, or clarify. Analysis-level operations include the following: identify parts, distinguish, diagram, outline, relate or associate, break down, discriminate, subdivide, analyze, separate, order, connect, classify, arrange, divide, select, infer, analyze, appraise, calculate, categorize, compare, contrast, compare and contrast, criticize, differentiate, discriminate, distinguish, examine, experiment, question, or test.
5. **Synthesize.** Put parts together to form a new whole. Synthesize-level operations include the following: combine, compose, create, design, redesign, rearrange, integrate, modify, substitute, plan, invent, formulate, prepare, generalize, or rewrite.
6. **Evaluation.** Use a given criteria to determine the value of a thing or quality of a product or performance. Evaluation-level operations include the following: appraise, criticize, compare and contrast, support, conclude, discriminate, find main points, infer, deduce, assess, decide, rank, grade, test, measure, recommend, convince, select, judge, discriminate, support, argue, choose compare, defend, estimate, judge, predict, rate, select, value, or evaluate.

An Example

For example, Mr. Cooper was teaching a lesson on the presidency of John Quincy Adams to his middle school social studies class. Using the action words from Level 6 of Bloom's taxonomy (evaluation), he designed the following activities and assignments: (a) make a case to support a statement related to the importance of Adams's postpresidency years, (b) define a criterion for an effective presidency and make a formal critique of Adams's presidency, (c) compare and contrast Adams's presidency to Jimmy Carter's, and (d) identify and describe the five most important accomplishments of Adams's presidency. You can use these action words to design questions, activities, and assignments for any class or subject area.

ENHANCING ENCODING AND RETRIEVAL

Described here are four strategies for enhancing the encoding and retrieval of knowledge from LTM.

Massed vs. Distributed Practice

Massed vs. distributed practice refers to the idea that we remember more if practice sessions are spread out or distributed over time (distributed practiced) instead of in a single session (massed practice) (Olson and Hergenhan, 2009; Ormand, 2012).

Mnemonic Devices

Mnemonic devices link new information to familiar words or letter patterns for easier retrieval from LTM. For example, to remember the four types of learning theories in this book, you could use the first letter of each word: neurological, behavioral, cognitive, and transformative (NBCT), then create a sentence to help you remember: *New baby cries tonight.* This will help you retrieve the names of the four types of theories. There are a variety of mnemonic devices that can be used. However, they have limited uses because memory is only part of learning, it is not the same thing as learning.

Imagery

In using imagery, students are asked to picture in their minds what is to be learned, what is learned, or what was learned. Generating mental images of what is to be learned is a form of elaborative encoding (Eggen and Kauchak, 2020). It also is a form of dual encoding, as students are encoding both semantic information and visual information. For example, Ms. Gonzalez was teaching a lesson about frogs. She ended her lesson by asking her second-grade students to imagine that they were a frog. She then used guided imagery to help them imagine the sights and sounds they would experience if they were living in a pond. She connected important terms and concepts from this lesson to this experience.

Elaboration

Elaboration was described in the chapter 10 as a method for extending short-tern memory. It also can be used as a strategy for encoding and retrieving information from LTM. Here you connect information to be remembered with something you already remember.

Chapter Twelve

Learning

This chapter examines three areas related to learning: (a) transfer, (b) massed vs. distributed practice, and (c) the importance of knowledge.

TRANSFER

Chapter 11 described inert knowledge as knowledge that cannot be retrieved or used. Inert knowledge also refers to knowledge that does not move outside the confines of a school or classroom. For learning to have value, transfer must occur. *Transfer* in this context refers to the ability to use new knowledge and skills beyond the particular context in which they were learned.

For example, Mr. Miller teaches grammar as part of his middle school language arts class. However, his goal here is not for students to be able to analyze and parse sentences, to identify predicates and participles, or to complete worksheets. His ultimate goal is for students' learning to transfer to real-life situations. He wants his students to be able to speak and write in ways that are grammatically correct in contexts other than his class. Transfer enables them to do just this. There are two types of transfer: low-road transfer and high-road transfer (Perkins and Salomon, 2012).

Low-Road Transfer

Load-road transfer is the automatic triggering of well-practiced routines that occurs in contexts or situations similar to that in which they were learned. This is generally associated with procedural knowledge (skills). *Hugging* is used for low-road transfer. This is where a skill is practiced many times in a variety of contexts and situations over time so that automaticity is achieved. This is commonly called drill and practice. Drill and practice are appropriate for low-level skills instruction in limited quantities. However, it should never be used as the sole form of instruction in any subject area, as this would not enable students to develop higher level reasoning and problem-solving skills.

For example, Ms. Lewis taught her fifth-grade students how to look for familiar word parts to identify unknown words while reading. Her goal was for students to be able to use this skill automatically as they read. To promote low-level transfer, she taught the skill initially using the elements of effective skills instruction (see chapter 9). Then she had students practice this skill in a variety of ways, in many situations, over time. Eventually, students were able to use this skill without thinking about it as they read in other contexts.

Coach Anderson wanted to teach his wrestlers to use a single-leg take-down to take opponents to the mat. First, he taught and demonstrated the most basic elements of the skill in the wrestling practice room. He then used guided practice to walk his wrestlers through each step of the skill. Next, he used drill and practice over many practices in a variety of situations so that his wrestlers overlearned the takedown. Finally, when his wrestlers encountered similar situations in an actual match, they did not have to think, they simply reacted.

High-Road Transfer

High-road transfer occurs when students understand the guiding principles of what they have learned and are then able to apply these principles in situations that are not exactly like the context in which they were first learned. Hugging using drill and practice will be of little use here. Instead, *bridging* is used for high-road transfer. Here, the new knowledge is first taught in ways that make the basic principles abundantly clear. Then, the teacher demonstrates how the principles are applied in a variety of situations. And finally, students are asked to envision or apply these principles in other contexts.

An example would be the theories described in this book. These all require high-road transfer to be of use. Often, when students encounter these theories for the first time as preservice teachers, they seem to hold little value. And since most preservice teachers have spent relatively little time in an actual classroom, there is little to connect them to life beyond the college classroom.

In order to promote transfer in her educational psychology course, Professor Taylor taught the basic elements of each learning theory so that her students could clearly see and understand the guiding principles behind each. She kept her explanations as simple as possible, highlighting the salient elements. Then she presented many examples of how these theories could be applied or reflected in different teaching and learning contexts. Finally, she asked her students to apply these principles by designing learning experiences that reflected the theories. She also had her students provide a theoretical justification for the use of a various policies, procedures, practices, and programs that students observed in video recordings. These all served to enhance the possibility that students would be able to use this theoretical knowledge in their own future teaching situations.

MASSED VS. DISTRIBUTED PRACTICE

Massed vs. distributed practice was described briefly in chapter 11 in terms of remembering things. This theory also applies to learning. We learn more and learn more deeply if learning sessions are spread out or distributed over time instead of in a single session (Doyle and Zakrajsek, 2013). For example, studying thirty minutes a day for four days is much more effective for learning than studying for two hours in a single day. This gives the brain a chance to make connections and integrate new information with knowledge already stored. Cramming the night before an exam is not an effective way to learn. Cramming may enable you to remember some things for a short time, but it does not lead to understanding. If you wish to learn more and study less, use distributed practice for studying.

THE IMPORTANCE OF KNOWLEDGE

Cognitive learning theories place great emphasis on what students know. Since learning involves connecting the new to the known, the more we know the better we are able to learn. This idea is repeated in many places throughout this book. Also, a well-organized body of knowledge in long-term memory (LTM) is important because it improves problem-solving, reasoning, reading comprehension, and our ability to learn (Goldstein 2008). Thus, an important part of any teacher's job is to help students develop an organized body of knowledge.

There are three types of knowledge. *Declarative knowledge* is knowledge related to ideas, descriptions, propositions, or concepts. For example, knowledge related to history or educational psychology would be declarative knowledge. *Procedural knowledge* is knowledge of how to do things. For example, knowing how to play a guitar, ride a bike, or plan a lesson would be procedural knowledge. The third type is *conditional knowledge*. This is knowing how and when to use declarative and procedural knowledge. Each is stored differently in LTM; thus each should be taught differently. This is why we use different types of lesson plans to teach different sorts of things (Johnson, 2017).

Novices and Experts

One of the differences between experts and novices in any field is an organized body of knowledge. Experts have acquired a great deal of knowledge related to their area of expertise. This knowledge is organized in LTM in ways that reflect a deep understanding of the subject matter. This organization helps them easily retrieve important aspects of knowledge when necessary with very little attention (*automaticity*). It also helps them notice patterns and use chunking when working with information in short-term memory (STM). In comparison, the knowledge base of novices in any area is shallow and disjointed.

Teaching Tips

Here are four tips for enhancing students' ability to develop an organized body of knowledge.

1. **Carefully plan your lessons.** Well-designed lessons present knowledge in an organized, structured fashion with activities that clearly link to the lesson purpose (Johnson, 2017). This makes it more likely that you will have a logical flow of events, it minimizes confusion, and it reduces the time students spend off-task. Also, it is much easier for students to make sense out of order than it is to make sense out of chaos.
2. **Show students the structure of material to be learned.** Seeing the structure of what is to be learned provides the learner a sense of the whole and the relationships among ordinate, subordinate, and superordinate items to be learned. In your teaching practice, this can be done using an *advanced organizer*. Advanced organizers show students the structure of or key points related to what is to be learned in advance of the lesson (see chapter 15).
3. **Make real-world connections.** Learning is more likely to transfer to real-world settings if real-world connections are made during the lesson. Here you would connect the knowledge and skills being learned to students' lives or situations. This could be something as simple as using students' names and experiences for math word problems, comprehension work, or daily oral language. Another example would be the use of problem-based learning (PBL). PBL imbeds real-life problems into the curriculum (Johnson, 2017) (see chapter 19).
4. **Activate relevant schemata.** Activating relevant schemata brings to consciousness those things students already know about the material to be learned. KWL is a strategy often used here. For example, before starting a lesson on amphibians, Ms. Martinez asks her second-grade

students what they know (K) about frogs and toads. As students raise their hands, she lists what they say on the board in a column. She then asks students what (W) they want to find out about amphibians. She lists this in a second column. After the lesson, she asks students what they learned (L) about amphibians. She lists this in a third column and asks students to make any necessary corrections to the K list.

Chapter Thirteen

Constructivist Learning Theory

CONSTRUCTIVISM

Constructivism is a theory of learning that falls under the superordinate category of cognitive psychology. As you read about constructivism, you will notice a great deal of overlap with other cognitive learning theories.

The Basics

Constructivist learning theory posits that learning is an active process that occurs when new knowledge and understanding are constructed based on what we already know (Ormrod, Anderman, and Anderman, 2020). Each of us then constructs a slightly different view of that knowledge (NRC, 2000). This is the essence of constructivism.

For example, as you read this chapter on constructivism you will use any related knowledge already contained in long-term memory (LTM), along with your own experiences as learners to help you construct a meaningful concept of what this theory might be. If you have an abundance of related knowledge and experiences, this will be fairly easy to do. If you have very little related knowledge and experiences, you will have to work a little harder to build a meaningful concept. And since no two human experiences are alike, no two conceptions of constructivism will be exactly the same.

Cognitive Constructivism vs. Social Constructivism

There are two slightly differing views of constructivism.

Cognitive constructivism aligns with Piaget's learning theory, which posits that curiosity drives learning. Knowledge construction here is an individual, internal process (Bozkurt, 2017). As described in an earlier chapter, a state of disequilibrium is created when what is in our head is not in alignment with what we experience. It is the need to establish equilibrium, to bring order to disorder, and to satisfy curiosity that drives learning. In other words, humans' natural inclination to make sense out of their environment is the basis for human learning.

The role of the teacher here would be to arouse curiosity. This is done by asking questions, identifying inconsistencies, and highlighting points of dissonance. The teacher would also design learning experiences that build on students' interests and align with their natural desire to find out about their world to the greatest extent possible.

Social constructivism aligns with Vygotsky's learning theory. Knowledge construction here places greater emphasis on the larger cultural context in which learning occurs (Beck, 2017). Social constructivism posits that knowledge is constructed through interaction with our social world. The *social world* is comprised of all the people and media with whom and which we interact. Here we internalize knowledge structures and ways of thinking that we encounter in the social world.

The role of the teacher here would be to present new knowledge in the context of common cultural constructs. The teacher would also promote social interaction and thinking around the subject matter by creating opportunities for students to interact with each other. This could occur through cooperative learning activities, project-based learning, or working in pairs. Also, the teacher could include purposeful, planned conversation bubbles within learning experiences.

A CONSTRUCTIVIST VIEW OF LEARNING

Here are some descriptors of learning that align with constructivist learning theory:

- **Learning is an active process.** It is not a passive process. It is something one must actively strive to do. You cannot be learned. You cannot be learned at. Nobody can learn you. Instead you must learn. To illustrate, if you are simply reading the words on this page without making any attempt to understand what the words might mean, it will be very hard for you to construct a meaningful concept of constructivism (or to learn). For learning to occur, you need to be actively engaged in constructing meaning. This means that as you read you need to do some or all of the following: (a) check for understanding, (b) identify interesting or important ideas, (c) make a conscious effort to connect this information to what you already know about teaching and learning, (d) pause every once in a while to see if what you are reading makes sense, (e) connect the information to your own experiences, and then (f) think about possible applications for this new knowledge.

- **Learning is a cognitive process.** Learning takes place inside the head as existing knowledge is used to make sense of new information. As such, we can measure and observe the effects of learning, but not learning itself. We can never fully account for the new knowledge structures that are created. Moreover, learning often goes far beyond what is taught and measured. This is because students use their background knowledge and experience to infer, fill in the blanks, and even add to or extend what is presented. Thus, the whole of what students learn is often far greater than the sum of the individual parts.

- **Learning is not a standardized process.** Humans are not standardized products. Our brains are all unique. We all learn in different ways. We also bring different knowledge and experiences to a learning situation. Since learning is so unstandardized, it is not logical to assume that we could standardized the teaching process. In other words, there is no singular approach, methodology, or set of teaching strategies that work best for all students.

- **Real learning is meaningful.** *Rote learning*, a very low quality of learning, is meaningless. This is when information is taken in but there are little or no connections to anything currently in LTM. Rote learning does not lead to understanding and is fairly useless. In order to understand new information or to create meaning, it must be connected to information that is already understood. This is called *meaningful learning.* As the name implies, meaningful learning makes sense and can be easily encoded, retrieved, and applied. And, the more connections a learner can make to known things, the more meaningful this new information becomes.

- **Social interaction facilitates learning.** Working or talking with others necessitates that you explain, verify, and question your own knowledge as well as that of others. Social interaction also provides a variety of perspectives and enables you to build on the understanding of others.

UNRELIABLE SCHEMATA

The idea that knowledge is constructed does not mean that there are not facts or constructs that are objectively reliable. Neither does this theory suggest that teachers are to accept whatever students say about something as being correct. Instead, constructivist learning theory states that knowledge is constructed using what is in our head to interpret and understand new information. Since no two people have cognitive structures that are exactly the same, each person creates slightly different views of reality. However, if one uses an unreliable schema to interpret new information, chances are that the new information will also be somewhat unreliable.

If a learner were to say, "Pigs can fly," constructivist learning theory does not advocate that a teacher reinforce that view. Instead, if students say or come to know something that is obviously not correct, the teacher might say something like, "That sounds interesting. Let's see if we can find some information to support that." Or, "People have varying ideas about that. How would we go about finding out what is true?" Or the teacher could create an inquiry project or use some other activity to support or reject a dualistic statement.

The point is this: Instead of always putting the onus on the teacher to be the arbiter of truth, students can be empowered by asking them to use critical thinking to find and evaluate information and then synthesize and communicate that information. These are examples of high-level cognitive operations that engage students in learning at much deeper levels deeply than simply being told something is right or wrong.

Chapter Fourteen

The Learning Theory of Jerome Bruner

BRUNER'S LEARNING THEORY

Jerome Bruner's (1915–2016) theory shares many common elements with other learning theories. A closer look at some of the basic elements of his theoretical framework are included here.

Some of the Basic Elements

Natural inclination

Like many theorists, Bruner recognized humans' natural desire to make sense out of their environment (Bruner, 1977). Learning is enhanced if lessons and educational experiences are aligned with this natural inclination.

Categories

When humans experience reality, the human brain naturally seeks to induce order on perceived fields. It does this by creating categories based on reoccurring patterns (Bruner, 1966). The term for this cognitive operation is *inductive analysis* (discussed a little later in this chapter). A *category* is a classification of objectives based on common properties.

Concepts

Learning is an active process in which learners construct new concepts based on their current conceptual knowledge. A *concept* here refers to a mental representation of a class of items or ideas within a category. A concept has defining attributes that describe the elements necessary for an entity to be an example of a concept. Instruction should be designed to enable learners to grasp the basic structure of concepts being taught (discussed next).

Simple-to-complex

Both skills and concepts should be taught in their simplest form first. This provides a platform with which to attach more sophisticated or complex versions of these skills and concepts later.

Whole-to-part instruction

When teaching skills and concepts, whole-to-part instruction is most effective, as it enables students to see how the individual parts relate to the whole (Lim, Reiser, and Olina, 2009). In other words, providing the big picture first gives students a context for learning the individual parts. This is like showing the picture of the complete jigsaw puzzle first so that students know where the individual pieces go. The opposite would be to present the individual pieces and expect students to put them together in order to see the big picture.

As an example of whole-to-part instruction, Ms. Lee was teaching her middle school students how to write. She first created writing activities and assignments that asked her students to use writing to describe their ideas (whole). Then she taught skills related to grammar and punctuation within the context of students' own writing (parts). The opposite of this (part-to-whole instruction) would be trying to teach writing by teaching just grammar and punctuation skills in isolation apart from students' own writing. This approach has not been shown to be very effective (Weaver, 2009).

All concepts at all levels

Bruner believed that the basic foundation of any subject can be taught in some intellectually honest form to any child at any stage of development if it is broken down at the appropriate level (Morris, 1978). Even the most complex subjects can be taught at the early primary grades if they are structured and presented in their most basic forms.

As an example, Mr. Brady was teaching a geology unit to his first-grade students. At this level it would not be developmentally appropriate to go into details about the types of rocks, their names and composition, and how they were formed. Instead, Mr. Brady taught his students some basic geological concepts along with the rudimentary skills of a geologist. He taught them that there are different types of rocks and that geologists put rocks into groups based on how they look and feel. Then he gave his students sets of rocks and asked them to put them into groups based on what they look like (inductive analysis). Lists were created to describe the attributes of the rocks (literacy). They created graphs to describe the numbers of rocks in each category (math). Students were given a map of the playground and asked to look for rocks and mark where they found them (mapping). Simple lab reports were written in large group to describe the process and what they found (science and literacy).

These activities provided the basic conceptual knowledge and skills related to geology as well as other subject areas (math, literacy, science, and social studies). And since Mr. Brady's elementary school used a spiral curriculum (discussed next), he knew his students would revisit and built upon these skill and concepts in successive years.

Spiral curriculum

A *curriculum* is systematic plan for instruction for each subject area that describes the specific knowledge and skills to be taught at each grade level. According to Bruner curriculums should be designed to revisit basic ideas, building upon them over time until students have a full understanding of them (Bruner, 1977). This is the essence of a *spiral curriculum*. Here key concepts and skills of academic disciplines are taught in the early grades. These same concepts and skills are revisited and learned at successively higher levels with more depth and breadth as students move through the grade levels (Johnson, 2009).

Inductive analysis

Inductive analysis involves the use of *inductive reasoning* to examine and put order to a field. Inductive reasoning is a cognitive operation in which broad generalizations are made based on specific observations (Johnson, 2000). In other words, data are observed, then generalized conclusions are drawn from the data. *Deductive reasoning* is a complimentary cognitive process where specific conclusions are made based on a broad set of data.

Whereas deductive reasoning proceeds step-by-step along a predetermined path to teach new concepts, inductive reasoning enables students to quickly perceive reoccurring patterns and construct a big conceptual picture. Bruner recommended inductive reasoning be used in the teaching of skills and concepts. Learning based on this type of thinking tends to be more meaningful and often goes beyond what is presented in the lesson (LeFrancois, 2006). *Discovery learning* (discussed later) is a pedagogical strategy that utilizes inductive reasoning.

Disciplined inquiry

Bruner wanted students to understand the principles that lead to the creation of the various academic disciplines. *Disciplined inquiry* can be used toward this end. This is when teachers use the tools and processes of the specific discipline to enable students construct knowledge. For example, Mr. Brady had his first-grade students use some of the tools of a geologist to discover the basic principles of that discipline.

DISCOVERY LEARNING

Discovery learning is a pedagogical strategy in which students are not presented with subject matter in its final form at the beginning of the lesson; instead they are first exposed to some sort of structured experience in order for them to inductively discover defining attributes, concepts, principles, skills, or processes (Johnson, 2017). Explicit instruction is then provided along the way as necessary. Discovery learning comes in a variety of forms with varying degrees of structure, all of which require careful planning. Bruner believed that this type of learning facilitates transfer and retention better than direct instruction, increases problem-solving, develops reasoning processes, and enhances motivation for learning (LeFrancois, 2006).

Designing a Discovery Learning Lesson

Discovery learning lessons always contain a certain amount of open-endedness in that students often discover things beyond the lesson's purpose. However, it is also explicitly defined in that there are specific skills or concepts that the teacher wants students to possess as a result of the learning experience. There are three basic parts to a discovery learning lesson.

First, the lesson begins with a discovery activity or experience of some sort in which students are able to discover important elements related to the lesson's purpose.

Second, after the discovery activity students are first asked to identify and describe those important elements noticed or learned. For example: "What did you notice about . . ." or, "What have you discovered about . . ." Students are then provided specific information related to the lesson's purpose. Here the teacher corrects misinformation, supplies any necessary missing information, and makes sure students get to the right conceptual place at the end of the lesson. Often the input is used to extend students' initial discoveries.

Third, the lesson ends with an independent practice activity. This is an activity or assignment designed to reinforce, practice, or apply what students have learned. Here students use or manipulate the lesson's content in some fashion.

Discovery Learning for Skills Instruction

As with direct instruction, discovery learning can be used to teach a skill. Here students are first immersed in an experience or activity in which they need to use the skill. Students should be given plenty of time and materials for experimenting. When students are ready for instruction, the teacher asks, "What have you discovered about [insert skill here]?" After listing students' ideas on the board, the teacher is then able to fill in the gaps and reinforce or extend upon what students have discovered.

A discovery learning skills lesson contains the three steps mentioned with the addition of guided practice. As described in chapter 9, you take the whole class through each step of the skill several times with a gradual release of teacher responsibility.

A Pedagogical Strategy

All teachers should know and be able to use discovery learning. However, like direct instruction, it is an instructional strategy, not a method of instruction. As such, it should never be used as the sole means of instruction for any subject. Also, while discovery learning may take a bit more time initially, students learn more deeply. This is because the instruction is based directly on what they have just experienced.

TEACHING CONCEPTS

Much of Bruner's work involved teaching concepts. Recall that a *concept* is a mental representation of a class of items or ideas within a category. Examples of concepts include freedom, empathy, mammal, interdependence, triangle, verb, theory, justice, or country.

Items within a concept share a set of essential characteristics called defining attributes. *Defining attributes* are the features required to make the entity a concept. For example, the defining attributes of a country are (a) it has recognized boundaries or borders, (b) it has a government that runs the country and provides certain public services such as education and police, (c) it has some sort of economy or system of money, and (d) it has sovereignty or makes decisions from within the country.

Effective concept instruction focuses first on the basic structure of the concept being taught. This enables learners to see the relationships between concepts, and it makes conceptual knowledge more easily retained and transferred. Also, understanding the basic structure of a concept helps students understand them at higher levels of complexity later. Both direct instruction and discovery learning should be used in teaching concepts.

Direct Instruction for Teaching Concepts

Direct instruction is a teacher-centered approach in which the information is presented to students in its final form. As with discovery learning, all teachers should know how and when to use direct instruction. Also, similar to discovery learning, direct instruction is a pedagogical strategy, not a method. It should never be used as the sole means of instruction. Here are the steps for using direct instruction to teach concepts:

1. **Present a definition of the concept.** The definition should use words and ideas with which students are familiar.
2. **Present the defining attributes of the concept.** Tell students that in order for that entity to be the concept it must have all of the defining attributes. *Concept maps,* sometimes called semantic maps, can be used here (Johnson, 2017). These are any type of visual representation of a concept that shows the relationship among ordinate and subordinate parts. Concept maps can be used during the teaching episode or as a post-lesson activity.
3. **Present positive examples of the concept.** Beginning teachers often err in providing too few examples. Students should be given many examples of the concept to be learned. (Think of three as the minimum number of examples to provide.) With each example, emphasize the defining attributes (tell why the concept is the concept).
4. **Present negative examples of the concept.** Students should be given some examples of things that are similar to, but are not the concept. Use the defining attributes to describe why each example is not the concept. (Remember that all the defining attributes must be present for the entity to be the concept.)
5. **Use guided practice to identify the concept.** Present both positive and negative examples to students. Ask them to identify each and tell why it is or is not the concept and provide feedback related to their responses. This acts as a type of formative assessment (assessment while learning is still forming) that tells you if you need to reteach any part of the concept lesson.
6. **Use independent practice to reinforce concept learning.** Here students practice what they have already learned related to the concept. Independent practice can be done individually or in small groups.

Discovery Learning for Teaching Concepts

Using discovery learning, students are asked to use inductive reasoning to determine the principles or defining attributes of a concept. These are the basic steps:

1. Provide students with several examples of the concept. Ask them if they can perceive any similarities or common attributes.

2. Provide nonexamples and ask students to compare to examples in order to note differences.
3. Ask students to identify the defining attributes of the concept.
4. Present the name and definition of the concept.
5. Make corrections or additions to students' list of defining attributes.
6. As a form of guided practice, ask students to identify other examples and nonexamples of the concept. They should be able to summarize principles or main concepts at this point.
7. Create a concept map or graphic organizer at the end of the lesson to describe the concept and the ordinate, superordinate, and subordinate relationships within that concept.

IT IS NOT A LEARNING THEORY

This chapter provided an overview of some of Jerome Bruner's big ideas. He is probably best known for discovery learning, the spiral curriculum, disciplined inquiry, and the teaching of concepts. One last note about discovery learning is that it is sometimes referred to as a learning theory. This is not quite correct. As already stated, it is a pedagogical strategy. Again, this is one of many strategies that all teachers should have in their teaching toolbox (Johnson, 2017).

Chapter Fifteen

Ausubel's Theory of Meaningful Verbal Learning

Like Jerome Bruner, David Ausubel (1918–2008) was a cognitive learning theorist who emphasized the importance of structure. You will see many common elements; however, the biggest difference between Bruner and Ausubel was Ausubel's emphasis of expository teaching over discovery learning.

MEANINGFUL VERBAL LEARNING THEORY

David Ausubel's theory of meaningful verbal learning emphasizes the importance of structure and the connection between new information and known. Whereas Bruner recommended discovery learning, Ausubel identified reception learning using expository teaching as the most effective method to use in helping students construct new knowledge (Ausubel, Novak and Hanesian, 1978).

Meaningful verbal learning

According to Ausubel, *meaningful verbal learning* occurs when new knowledge is received directly from the teacher in a form in which students can receive it (Ausubel, Novak and Hanesian, 1978). Here, the structure of what is to be learned is clearly evident and students are able to see how new knowledge connects to what they already know. The teacher's job is to use expository teaching (see the next bullet) to present this new information in ways that enable learners to see the structure and make these connections.

Expository teaching

Expository teaching is when the content to be learned is presented to students in its final form using direct instruction (Good and Brophy, 1995; LeFrancois, 2006). This is a transmission approach to teaching that is highly teacher-centered and lecture-oriented. According to Ausubel, expository teaching is the most effective method to use for meaningful verbal learning (Ausubel, 1977).

Students' knowledge

The most important factor influencing students' learning of new knowledge is the quantity, clarity, and organization of their present knowledge (Ausubel and Robinson, 1969). As previously stated, new knowledge must connect to what students already know for meaningful verbal learning to occur. Thus, when teaching new concepts or skills, teachers need to have a sense of what students already know.

Organized bodies of information

For meaningful verbal learning to occur, new information must be organized hierarchically so the structure is readily apparent (Ausubel and Robinson, 1969). The structure of this new information serves two purposes. First, it acts as a scaffold to organize and hold information as students are creating or expanding cognitive structures. Students are able to see the hierarchical nature of the new information and its relationships to existing cognitive structures. Second, the structure of the new information serves as a scaffold for retrieval. Even if details are forgotten, students will be able to retrieve the basic structure and remember key ideas associated with the structure.

As an example, this book makes ample use of headings and subheadings. This structure enables readers to quickly see and more easily encode the content within each chapter.

Advanced organizers

Expository teaching should begin with an advanced organizer (explained in the next section).

Advanced Organizers

Advanced organizers are any form of visual, verbal, or written material that depicts the structure of the content to be learned. They provide an overview of what is to be learned in advance of the learning episode. According to Ausubel (1977), advanced organizers have three main purposes.

- **Highlight key points.** Advanced organizers can be used to direct students' attention to the important parts of the upcoming lesson. This gives students the big picture and enables them to put new facts and concepts in a meaningful context.
- **Activate relevant knowledge**. Advanced organizers also can be used to remind students of the relevant knowledge they already know. This helps students make the connections between the known and the new.
- **Show relationships.** Finally, advanced organizes can be used to show the relationship between important points described in the upcoming input. Put another way, advanced organizers are designed to show students the superordinate, ordinate, and subordinate relationship between and within key concepts.

Advanced organizers take a variety of forms including: (a) an outline; (b) a quick verbal overview that identifies the main points to be learned; (c) a picture or graphic that shows the concept's superordinate, ordinate, and subordinate parts; (d) a semantic map or concept map, (e) concrete models; (f) analogies; (g) a discussion of the main themes or ideas; (h) a set of defining attributes or higher order rules; (i) Venn diagrams or comparison charts, and (j) a short abstract or summary of material to be learned or read. Again, to be effective advanced organizers should clearly show the structure of the material to be learned (Johnson, 2017).

Lectures: The Importance of Expository Teaching

Expository teaching is a teacher-centered form of direct instruction in which students receive information directly from a teacher using some form of lecture (Johnson, 2017). Effective expository teaching is one of many pedagogical strategies that all teachers should possess. As well, it is appropriate for use at all levels as long as the duration is developmentally appropriate. As described in chapter 2, human attention is limited. Eric Jensen (2005) identified the appropriate duration for lecture at five levels:

- Grades K–2: 5–8 minutes
- Grades 3–5: 8–12 minutes
- Grades 6–8: 12–15 minutes
- Grades 9–12: 12–15 minutes
- Adults: 15–18 minutes

This does not mean that lessons should not go longer than the durations identified above. Instead lessons using expository teaching should consist of small bits of direct instruction that are briskly paced with some sort of a pause and process activity between (Johnson, 2016). The strategy could be as simple as, "Turn to a neighbor and share one good idea."

Here are two examples to illustrate this. First, Mr. Gonzalez was teaching a unit on birds to his first-grade class as part of the science curriculum. He wanted his students to have some basic knowledge related to birds. A lesson plan was used to organize the information he would teach in the learning episode. This lesson plan enabled him to see the structure and sequence of the information he would provide. Before the lesson he put a diagram with labels on the board to use as an advanced organizer. He used expository teaching and lots of pictures to give information to his students in two- to five-minute teaching episodes. Each teaching episode was followed by a very short activity where his students physically mimicked some aspect of the bird information he was teaching. His science class consisted of two of these teaching episodes followed by a longer activity related to birds.

Second, Professor Nelson gave a lecture on cognitive learning theories in her university educational psychology course. She put an outline on the board before the class to use as an advanced organizer. She quickly went over the advanced organizer before the class. Her students were able to see the structure and sequence of the material she would be teaching that day. The advanced organizer also acted as a scaffold to enhance her students' ability to encode and retrieve this new information. Her lecture was well planned and replicated the structure of the advanced organizer. During the lecture she set a timer for fifteen minutes. Every fifteen minutes she paused briefly and asked students to do something like, "Share an interesting or important idea with a neighbor," "Write down one idea that seems to stand out," "Share with a neighbor an idea how this might be like something else you know," or "Describe an example of this you have encountered." These brief breaks enabled students to pause and process this new information, hear the thoughts of others, and make connections to what they know or had experienced.

EXPOSITORY TEACHING

Expository teaching is a form of direct instruction, the goal of which is to connect new information with learners' existing knowledge. These are the steps of expository teaching using an advanced organizer:

1. **Advanced organizer.** Start the lesson with an advanced organizer that previews the general principles to be learned. Briefly describe the purpose of the lesson and alert students to important key concepts.
2. **Input.** Present the information students must know. The new material should be presented in an organized fashion and logically sequenced.

Signaling techniques should be used to call learners' attention to how the new information relates to the advanced organizer. Student questions should be elicited at each step in order to promote active learning and ensure mastery.

3. **Review.** Finish the lesson by reviewing the main points, again referencing the advanced organizer.

4. **Extend and apply.** Finally, include an activity or assignment that requires students to describe the newly learned material in their own words, or ask them to apply or extend the information in new contexts.

COMPARING DIRECT INSTRUCTION AND DISCOVERY LEARNING

Is expository teaching using direct instruction more effective than discovery learning? In the book *Visible Learning and the Science of How We Learn* (2014), authors John Hattie and Gregory Yates compared discovery learning with direct instruction and concluded that direct instruction is effective and discovery learning is not. Let us unpack their conclusions.

A Meta-Analysis

First, the comparison of discovery learning and direct instruction was a result of a meta-analysis. One of the limitations of a meta-analysis when used in education is that there are a number of unaccounted variables and thus a certain lack of validity. For example, when comparing discovery learning and direct instruction, we do not know how achievement was defined in the various studies as well as what was measured and how it was measured. We also do not know how discovery learning and direct instruction were defined and implemented in any of the classrooms in these studies. And finally, we know nothing about the teachers, the students, the comparison groups, and their environments. Indeed, this is why Hattie stated in an earlier book that a meta-analysis and effect size should be a place to begin the discussion, but not an endpoint for making decisions (Hattie, 2012).

Putters and Drivers

To say that direct instruction is more effective than discovery learning misses the point: They are both pedagogical strategies used for different purposes. To use a golfing analogy, this would be like saying that a driver is more effective than a putter. While the ball may go farther when hit with a driver, trying to putt with it would be ineffective.

Method or Strategy

In their comparison Hattie and Yates did not differentiate between a method and a strategy. A method in education usually refers to a defined process or specific set of techniques that are used exclusively in a prescribed fashion for all instruction in a particular subject area. A pedagogical strategy is a specific teaching technique that is adopted and adapted for selective use in all subject areas for a specific purpose.

Direct instruction and discovery learning, when effectively implemented, are both pedagogical strategies, not methods of instruction. Neither of these strategies should be utilized exclusively as the sole means of instruction for teaching anything for any population. There are instances when each is the most effective strategy to use. What's more, it is not an either/or assertion. Often discovery learning and direct instruction are included in the same lesson.

Effective Golfers and Teachers

As stated in various places in this book, master teachers have a variety of pedagogical strategies in their teaching toolbox. They know how and when to use each and for what purpose. Indeed, the effectiveness of any strategy is dependent on how it is used and for what purpose. Just as an effective golfer has many clubs and knows how and when to use each one, effective teachers know how to use both direct instruction and discovery learning.

Part V

Transformative Learning Theories

The next four chapters examine learning theories that can be described as transformative. They have at their core the belief that true learning involves change or some form of growth at one's deepest levels.

- Chapter 16: Humanistic Learning Theory
- Chapter 17: Applying Humanistic Learning Theory in the Classroom
- Chapter 18: Holistic Learning Theory
- Chapter 19: Applying Holistic Learning Theory in the Classroom

Chapter Sixteen

Humanistic Learning Theory

Psychologists Carl Rogers (1902–1987) and Abraham Maslow (1908–1970) are generally thought to be the founders of modern humanistic learning theory (DeCarvalho, 1991). Humanistic learning theory is not as easily defined as some of the other theories described in this book. Indeed there are differing views on what humanistic learning theory is or might be. And like other learning theories described in this book, they share common elements.

However, all views on humanistic learning seem to share three overriding tenets. First, humans are by their very nature evolving, self-developing creatures. As such, we have a natural inclination to learn and develop fully. Second, learning is enhanced when educational experiences align with these natural desires. And third, the goal of education should be to enable each person to develop his or her full potential.

HUMANISTIC EDUCATION

Humanistic learning theory is the theory upon which *humanistic education* is based. These terms are used interchangeably in this chapter.

Dehumanizing Education

Humanistic education is in essence a reaction to an educational system that is seen as dehumanizing. These dehumanizing elements include the following:

- Students are often asked to be passive learners or to learn in ways that are not natural for them. As well, the things given to them to learn are often meaningless or have no connection to their lives and experiences.

- Manipulation is often used to get students to learn and to behave in acceptable ways. Instead of building on their natural inclinations, students are manipulated by external rewards and punishment to "learn" school-related things and be compliant. What is rarely considered are the reasons why students may not want to learn or why their behaviors may be negative or disruptive.
- One-dimensionality is perpetuated. Only the cognitive dimension of students' humanity is recognized. Ignored in classrooms and curriculum are the many aspects that make us human: our creativity, imagination, curiosity, social natures, and emotional dimensions.
- Humans and human learning are too often described only in terms of numbers. Experiences, traits, endeavors, and achievements that cannot be quantified are thought not to exist or to be of little value. This quantification of the educational experience is often used to compare students to a mythical norm. Such quantification creates winners and losers as students find themselves above or below a mythical "average."
- Only traditional knowledge and ways of knowing and being in the world are seen to be of worth. Views that do not align with traditional perspectives are seen as less important. Norms and values that do not reflect the dominant culture are diminished or ignored. And only the history that tells the story of advantaged groups is seen as being worth repeating.

Goals

Humanistic education views learning in terms of personal growth and the development of each person's full potential. Growth and development occur here, not just on an intellectual level, but also on an emotional, psychological, creative, social, and physical level (DeCarvalho, 1991; Maslow, 1971; Morris, 1978; Rogers and Freiberg, 1994; Patterson, 1973). Within this context, five goals are identified:

1. Facilitate the development of fully functioning, self-actualized human beings who have the capacity to nurture themselves, others, and their environment.
2. Instill a joy of learning and a desire to be life-long learners.
3. Promote the discovery of each student's passions, special talents, and abilities.
4. Teach the knowledge and skills necessary for students to be good decision-makers and effective problem-solvers.
5. Enable students to be responsible world citizens who are able to contribute to democratic societies.

Two Misconceptions

Two common misconceptions about humanistic education are addressed:

1. **Humanistic education is not secular humanism.** This is a definition of secular humanism.

   > *Secular humanism is a way of thinking and living that aims to bring out the best in people so that all people can have the best in life. Secular humanists reject supernatural and authoritarian beliefs. They affirm that we must take responsibility for our own lives and the communities and world in which we live. Secular humanism emphasizes reason and scientific inquiry, individual freedom and responsibility, human values and compassion, and the need for tolerance and cooperation* (Counsel for Secular Humanism, 2006).

   In contrast, humanistic education embraces a wide range of reasoning and types of inquiry. Also, humanistic learning theory has nothing to say about religion or "supernatural" beliefs. As a theory, it neither dismisses nor embraces any form of religion or any aspect related to spirituality.

2. **Humanistic education does not dismiss or diminish academic learning.** Indeed when correctly implemented, humanistic education complements and enhances academic learning, intellectual growth, and the development of academic skills. This occurs by making personal connections with the curriculum to students' lives and experiences (to the greatest extent possible). Thus students learn more and learn more deeply. In other words, academic learning enables students to develop the knowledge and skills necessary to thrive in the world as well as provides a context for personal growth.

HUMANISTIC LEARNING THEORY

This section defines humanistic learning theory and presents supporting principles.

Defining Humanistic Learning Theory

Humanistic learning theory recognizes that humans have a natural tendency to evolve, grow, learn, and develop fully. Carl Rogers described this as an instinctive inner core that moves people toward reaching their full potential (Rogers, 1969). Abraham Maslow (1968) used the term *self-actualization* to describe humans' innate, natural progression toward their highest state.

Learning is enhanced when educational experiences align with these natural desires.

Humanistic learning theory explains learning as movement toward self-actualization that occurs as a result of instruction or experience. Such learning occurs in furtherance of students' predisposition and ability toward becoming good decision-makers, effective problem-solvers, and responsible world citizens who contribute to democratic societies.

Supporting Principles

Humanistic learning theory is based on five supporting principles.

1. **Students' learning should be as self-directed as possible.** In other words, students should be given choices about what they learn, how they learn, and how they demonstrate their learning, to the greatest degree possible. Choice here does not mean total choice all the time. Instead it means as much choice as is appropriate for the situation. Choice exists on a continuum. For example, you can offer:

   • No choice: "We're studying the Civil War this month. This is the book we're going to read. This is the topic you'll be doing reports on."
   • A choice within a set: "I've put out five books for you. You can choose the one you wish to read."
   • A choice within a category: "We're studying the Civil War this month. You can read any book or investigate any topic related to the Civil War."
   • Total choice: "Find a topic that interests and inspires you for your research project. These are the criteria. This is the due date. Find a book that you love for our reading class."

   Some situations require more choice, some less choice. The goal is to provide the minimum amount of control necessary to create a positive learning experience.

2. **The subject matter to be learned should be relevant to the lives or personal interests of the students.** It should be connected to the students' lives or interests whenever possible and to the greatest extent possible. For example, when learning number facts in the primary grades, students would be asked to use them to figure out problems in real-life situations. Humanistic educators find creative ways for mandated subject matter to reflect or connect with students' lives. At the same time, space is provided within a curriculum for students to explore topics of interest to them. For example, knowing what is of

interest to adolescents, humanistic educators would seek to incorporate themes related to social experiences, relationships, and defining roles and values into traditional subject areas.

3. **The full spectrum of the human experience should be included in the educational experience.** Emotions, relationships, creativity, imagination, and real-life problems are all part of the human experience. Including them in the educational experience enhances learning as well as the development of humans. Humanistic educators create the conditions where human beings can learn to use all these human dimensions to solve problems, make decisions, and come to know the world. As well, traditional curriculums are studied in a multidimensional context. Art, drama, music, poetry, creative writing, and other arts are used as tools along with traditional methods to explore or respond to information and ideas.

4. **Schools should produce students who want to learn and know how to learn.** Humanistic educators build on students' natural desire to learn by asking them to learn about things that are relevant to their lives and by helping them to make the connections. Curriculums are designed around students' natural ways of learning and include things about which students want to learn. As well, students are taught how to learn. That is, how to get the necessary information they need, how to critically analyze and evaluate that information, and how to use and apply the information.

5. **Students learn best in a nonthreatening environment.** Threats come in the form of physical threats, but also social threats, emotional threats, or things that endanger one's self-esteem or phenomenological self (Combs, 1999). These types of threats occur when schools focus more on measuring learning than they do on enhancing learning.

Chapter Seventeen

Applying Humanistic Learning Theory in the Classroom

Chapter 16 described some of the basic elements of humanistic learning theory. This chapter describes how these elements might be applied in a classroom setting.

THE HUMANISTIC EDUCATOR

Carl Rogers described three teacher traits that are necessary for learning (Rogers and Freiberg, 1994):

1. **Respect.** Teachers respect each student, using what Rogers (1961) calls unconditional positive regard (UPR). Here, students are accepted for who they are, without conditions. Note that this is much different than accepting unacceptable behavior. This type of respect for students helps to promote their own self-respect and sense of self-efficacy, which in turn enhances learning.

2. **Empathetic understanding.** Teachers strive to see things from the student's point of view. They understand what it feels like to be excited, lost, confused, proud, frustrated, curious, anxious, confident, or bored. They also know what it feels like to have a teacher who cares for them, who is rooting for them to succeed, who believes that they are of worth and can accomplish things.

3. **Genuineness or congruence.** Teachers teach from their authentic self. They are not playing a role or projecting what they believe a teacher should be. Rather their teaching persona is in congruence with who they are. In addition, what is taught and how they teach it are in

congruence with their principles. Genuine teachers do not have to rely on methods or techniques; instead they can trust their own values, knowledge, and experiences to guide them.

According to the humanistic educator, once these three conditions are met, then learning can begin.

EDUCATION AS SELF-ACTUALIZATION

For the humanistic educator, schools are vehicles for self-actualization. *Self-actualization* has two parts. First, one is able to accept and express one's inner core or self, and second, one begins to actualize those capacities and potentialities found there (Maslow, 1968). There are four tasks specifically related to self-actualization:

1. **Discover and understand oneself.** This occurs through writing and various other self-reflective experiences. Understanding and accepting oneself makes it more likely that one can understand and accept others. Part of self-actualizing then involves integrating the conscious and unconscious parts of one's personality (Russel-Chapin, Rybak, and Copilevitz, 1996). It also involves recognizing and understanding one's emotional self. Only by bringing unconscious emotions to consciousness is one free to act upon them.
2. **Express one's inner core.** Once one has encountered significant emotions, images, and ideas from intrapersonal dimensions, the next step is to express them. This expression allows these entities to interact with other humans, and in so doing, creates a more dynamic and more richly defined interaction between the unconscious and conscious mind. This can be done through poetry, writing, music, dance, the visual arts, and drama, as well as in small group discussions where students are engaged in honest dialogue.
3. **Find one's passion and act on it.** This is a matter of first discovering a topic or an area about which one is passionate, and then fully exploring or embracing it. This is what mythologist Joseph Campbell (1968) calls finding your bliss. For example, a student may find a passion for science, mathematics, religion, marketing, writing, or some more specific topic. Humanistic educators find spaces within a school curriculum where students are allowed to pursue areas of interest. Part of a teacher's role then is to expose students to a wide variety of topics and create the structure whereby they can indulge their passions.
4. **Discover one's strengths or particular talents and learn how to use them to solve problems.** Highly successful people are not necessarily

those who have a great many strengths and few weaknesses; rather, successful people are those who learn how to use their strengths to compensate for a weakness in order to solve problems or create products (Sternberg, 1996). Too often students (especially students who are struggling learners) are defined and described in terms of what they cannot do or how far their scores fall from a mythical average. Humanistic educators see their role as helping students to discover what they can do, developing their talents, and then using those talents to become effective problem-solvers.

SELF-ACTUALIZATION ACTIVITIES

Self-actualization activities and assignments need not (and should not) replace curriculums already in place. Like a small glove inside a larger one, these types of activities and assignments can augment and enhance those things a teacher is already doing. Self-actualizing activities should have some or all of the following characteristics:

1. **They are open-ended.** Students are not always expected to come to a predetermined conclusion or create a standardized product. Like in life, there is often not a set answer. Students are allowed and even encouraged to come to their own conclusions. Also, in creating, responding, writing, and discussing they can take an idea as far as they want or, in turn, respond as minimally as they feel necessary.

   For example, you would not find a teacher saying to a student, "Your writing assignment is very short. Why don't you go back and add some more description?" Instead the teacher would say, "Very good. What else do you want to write about today?"

2. **They are meaningful.** Assignments and activities are not created to keep students busy, to have them regurgitate their knowledge for the teacher, or to get a dispersion of scores. Rather, self-actualization activities are designed to increase students' understanding or to move them forward in some way. This means that they are able to connect the activity or assignment with something they know or have experienced.

   For example, after reading a chapter in a text, instead of doing some sort of worksheet to reinforce ideas or to gage their comprehension, a humanistic educator might say, "Find an idea or event that you find interesting. Describe it using words, pictures, or some other form, then tell us how it might connect with something you know or have experienced."

3. **They connect with students' lives.** These activities try to make connections with students' inner or outer lives. For example, after reading a story, students might be asked to describe similar feelings, events, characters, or situations from their own lives. In a science lesson, students might be directed to see how a concept touches their lives or to take an imaginary trip somewhere and describe what they see, feel, hear, and even smell.

4. **They promote a greater understanding of self.** One of the goals self-actualization activities is to examine those parts of ourselves that have been ignored. This is done in order to begin to recognize why we think and feel as we do. This would include reflective activities or assignments in which emotional, intuitive, social, or other intrapersonal elements are examined.

5. **They promote a greater understanding of others.** Activities and assignments here enable students to look beyond surface differences, to see the commonalities of the human experience. These surface differences often include areas such as ability, race, ethnicity, culture, socioeconomic status, and religion. This deeper look helps students connect with others in a more meaningful way.

6. **They allow students to share their ideas with others**. Here the teacher creates structured spaces within the curriculum for students to share their thoughts and ideas with others. As well, students are asked to respond to the ideas of others. Activities and assignments here might include cooperative learning activities, discussion groups, oral communication activities, or a variety of inquiry projects and presentations (Johnson, 2017). This could also include things such as asking students to turn to a neighbor to get help or to share an idea, author's chair, or aesthetic responses to classmates' writing or other academic products and performances.

7. **They recognize multiple ways to demonstrate knowing.** In traditional curriculums, knowledge is often demonstrated only by taking a test or writing a report. Self-actualizing activities and assignments instead invite people to express their knowledge and understanding in a variety of ways. For example, students may create dramas to demonstrate important concepts, use art or photography, give a speech, use dance or creative movement, use music, do inquiry or problem-solving projects, use poetry or creative writing, or create a video.

USE AS APPROPRIATE

Humanistic educators would not suggest that every activity or assignment be self-actualizing. Instead these types of activities and assignments should be inserted within curriculums only as appropriate.

Chapter Eighteen

Holistic Learning Theory

HOLISM AND INTERCONNECTEDNESS

Holistic learning theory is the theory upon which *holistic education* is based. These terms are used interchangeably in this chapter. Like humanistic learning theory, there are many views on what holistic learning theory is or might be. This chapter provides an overview of some of the common elements.

Theory of Holism

Holism is derived from the word *holon*. A holon is something that is simultaneously a whole and a part. That is, each little part contains the whole within. For example, the smallest bit of physical matter contains the building blocks for the universe in the same way that each individual cell in our body carries the DNA of the whole person.

The theory of holism is based on the concept of a holon. This theory states that the universe and all entities within are made up of integrated parts that cannot exist independently of the whole. As such, we can never come to know the whole of reality by isolating variables in order to examine small parts. In other words, science cannot understand how the universe works by taking it apart in the same way one would take apart a mechanical clock. Instead, universes and all the entities within them are a system of systems in which the parts interact and interconnect with each other. As such, the whole is much more than the sum of its parts. Thus, any entity (universe, human, school, student, classroom, curriculum, concept, or subject matter) is best understood by examining the principles that govern behavior within the system. That is the theory of holism.

Interconnectedness

Holistic learning theory is based on the theory of holism. There are differing views of what holistic learning theory is or might be; however, one unifying principle is the interconnectedness of all things (Clark, 1991). This is the same principle of interconnectedness that is found in the field of quantum physics, where all things in the physical universe are said to be interconnected at the quantum level (Al-Khalili, 1999; Talbot, 1991). *Quantum* is a term used to denote the smallest physical unit or thing that can still be recognized. At this level there is no fragmentation, only parts that are interconnected within greater systems and greater wholes.

The idea of interconnectedness is also illustrated in *systems theory*, which views the universe and all things within it in terms of interconnected systems (Von Bertalanffy, 1968). According to this theory, reality is a unified whole comprised of self-organizing systems that are both interactive and interdependent. This is why it is said that a butterfly fluttering its wings on one side of the globe can cause a hurricane on the other side. Any change in one entity or part of the system will bring change in all. Thus, all entities within this reality should be perceived in terms of patterns, connections, interconnections, and relationships all interconnected and influencing each other.

The idea of interconnectedness can also be illustrated in Carl Jung's concept of the collective unconscious (Jung, 1938). The *collective unconscious* is a part of the human psyche that is shared by all (Jones, 1999). Here every thought, action, and emotion ever experienced by humanity is embedded and available to us in the form of archetypal images. *Archetypal images* are those images formed around patterns within in the collective unconscious and birthed into human consciousness as symbols and motifs (Pearson, 1989).

Carl Jung (1938) described a common set of archetypal images that appear in mythology, fairy tales, stories, literature, dreams, art, and religions throughout the world. These help us understand the nature of our existence in the physical world and our place in the cosmos. They can also be used as guides on our inner journey toward *oneness of consciousness*. This oneness, also called *individuation*, is an integration of the conscious and unconscious mind that leads to self-actualization (Jones, 1999).

TO EDUCATE

Educate comes from the Latin word *educere*, which means "to draw forth." To *educe,* the root derivative of *educate*, is to bring out something of potential that is latent or indwelling. For holistic educators, ultimate truth resides within each individual. Knowledge and skills are seen as a means toward this end (ultimate truth), and not an end in and of themselves. Holistic educators then teach knowledge and skills with the goal of bringing out and developing qualities that are inherent within each student. And just like humanistic educators, holistic educators perceive all humans as having a natural desire to learn and a tendency to evolve to their highest states.

Transformational Learning and Teaching

From a holistic perspective, true learning is said to have occurred when educational experiences elicit a transformation of *consciousness*. This transformation, in turn, leads to a greater understanding of and care for self, others, and one's environment. Consciousness here is that of what we are aware, both internally and externally. Learning can thus be expressed in terms of personal transformation as it relates to the expansion of consciousness. We can transform ourselves and ultimately the world around us by transforming consciousness. This transformation can occur internally by noticing greater dimensions of self and externally by perceiving the interconnection of all things.

For example, we have within us both evolving and devolving traits. The evolving traits are those that serve to enhance our growth. These are traits such as humility, love, self-respect, fortitude, concentration, diligence, equanimity, and nonviolence. The devolving elements are traits that impede our growth. These are traits such as anger, greed, hatred, ignorance, pride, and self-centeredness. Evolving and devolving traits create emotional states from which thoughts arise. Since thought in some form precedes action, educational experiences that enable students to develop the evolving traits are an important part of helping them transform into beings who are better able to nurture self, others, and their environment.

Transformation also occurs during learning experiences in which students and a teacher are engaged in what Abraham Maslow (1968) called *peak experiences*. Here there is a change in consciousness as both the teacher and students have an intense focus and total attention to the moment. There is a sense of knowing that goes beyond the lesson and a distortion in the perception of time. One senses interconnectedness, where the borders between self and the universe seem to dissolve. Here the teacher and learner become one as both are transformed by the experience. These types of experiences do not occur often; however, master teachers can describe them. And, as master teachers gain additional knowledge and experience, these types of experiences occur more frequently.

Defining Holistic Learning Theory

Holistic learning theory recognizes the interconnectedness of all human dimensions including intellectual, emotional, physical, social, imaginative, and transpersonal dimensions. Real learning is said to have occurred only when all dimensions are addressed. Holistic learning theory also recognizes the interconnectedness of all things, including self, others, and one's environment. Recognizing this interconnectedness, holistic learning theory identifies intelligent acts as those that would nurture or give to self, others, and one's environment. Unintelligent acts would be those that break down such interconnectedness by harming or taking from self, others, or one's environment.

Based on the ideas described here, a definition of holistic learning theory would be a theory that explains learning as a change in consciousness that occurs as a result of instruction, experience, or reflection that in turn leads to the furtherance of intelligent acts. Intelligent acts are those that serve to nurture and give to self, others, and one's environment.

Essential Characteristics of Holistic Education

Holistic education has its historical origin in the work of Rudolph Steiner, John Dewy, and Maria Montessori. Here are six essential characteristics:

1. **Holistic education nurtures the development of the whole person.** Like humanistic education, holistic education seeks to help students grow and develop in all dimensions: intellectual, emotional, physical, social, imaginative, and transpersonal dimensions. However, unlike humanistic education, holistic education recognizes the transpersonal element (see number 5).
2. **Holistic education promotes relationships.** These relationships can occur between learners, teachers, people in the community, or people living in other parts of the world. Holistic education values any type of interpersonal connection that can be used to enhance learning. In a school or classroom, holistic educators move away from authoritarian, top-down relationships based on power and authority and toward more equal relationships based on principles of respect and a shared set of values. Instead of using power to control students, relationships are used to invite students to cooperate in creating an effective learning environment and meaningful learning experiences.
3. **Holistic education seeks to incorporate real-life experiences with learning.** Instead of studying an abstract, academic world defined by somebody else, learning is linked to students' lives to the greatest extent possible. This include things like experiential learning or service learning in which real-world problems, experiences, and situations are infused into the curriculum and used as the basis of students' learning.
4. **Holistic education enables learners to critically examine and define their own values and views.** Students' learning includes experi-

ences in which they are able to critically examine established ways of thinking, seeing, and knowing. The purpose of these reflective examinations is to enable students to identify and then begin to internalize their own views and values.

5. **Holistic education recognizes the transpersonal element.** The transpersonal element is the part of self that transcends the self (Tart, 1996). It provides access to a complete range of conscious states and enables perception of the seamless connection between self, others, and the universe, sometimes known as *oneness*. This experience of oneness is what Buddhists sometimes call *the ground of being* (Hanh, 1998), or what quantum physicists call *implicate reality* (Goswami, Reed and Goswami, 1993). Here you see yourself as one living being in the context of all of life, and you see all of life in the context of one living being.

6. **Holistic education recognizes the interconnectedness of all things.** As already stated, reality can be perceived in terms of systems in which everything within each system is connected to and interconnected with all other things, including those within all other systems.

Connections

A holistic education framework is based on the principle of interconnectedness. It uses the curriculum and other educational experiences as vehicles to develop three kinds of connections: intrapersonal, interpersonal, and transpersonal.

1. **Intrapersonal connections.** Curriculum and other educational experiences are used to connect with and understand the central self. The *central self* is the part of you beyond the ego that some might call the *transpersonal self.* Intrapersonal connections can help students understand themselves, solve problems, make decisions, and come to know the world using intuition and emotion in conjunction with knowledge and logic.

2. **Interpersonal connections.** Curriculum and other educational experiences are used to connect with and understand others. Interpersonal connections can help students develop social and other interpersonal skills with the goal of understanding and learning to live in relationship or harmony with others.

3. **Transpersonal connections.** Curriculum and other educational experiences are used to perceive and understand the world in terms of interrelated systems and interconnected experiences. This might take the form of global education, where students see how their daily lives affect or connect with others around the world. This might also take

the form of ecological education, where students describe their impact on and relationship with the environment. Transpersonal connections invite students to be fully in relationship with themselves, others, and local and world communities, and to see and experience the interrelationship of all things.

ALL THEORIES CAN INFORM YOUR PRACTICE

Holistic educators perceive the ultimate purpose of our schools to be the transformation of students, teachers, and, ultimately, society and the world (Miller, 2000; Palmer, 1993; Nava, 2001; Nakagawa, 2002). This chapter provided just a brief overview of holistic learning theory and holistic education. No single theory is all-encompassing. Holistic learning theories, like all theories in this book, should not be adopted to the exclusion of other learning theories. All these theories can be used to inform your teaching practice.

Chapter Nineteen

Applying Holistic Learning Theory in the Classroom

This chapter describes examples of how some aspects of holistic learning theory might be applied or manifest in the classroom. These ideas are organized around the six essential characteristics of holistic education that were described in chapter 18. However, many of the ideas apply to more than one characteristic.

THE WHOLE PERSON

Essential characteristic #1: Holistic education nurtures the development of the whole person.

This includes intellectual, emotional, social, physical, and transpersonal dimensions. Here are some basic ideas for addressing the emotional and social dimensions.

Emotional Dimension

Emotional intelligence (EI) is a theory that defines intelligence as the ability to perceive, understand, and manage one's own emotions, to monitor the emotions of others, and to use that information to guide one's thinking and actions (Goleman, 1995; Pfeiffer, 2000). EI involves abilities that can be categorized into five domains:

- **Self-awareness:** The ability to observe yourself and recognize a feeling as it happens (intrapersonal intelligence).

- **Managing emotions:** The ability to (a) handle feelings so they are appropriate, (b) understand the origin of emotions, and (c) find ways to handle negative emotions (fears, anxieties, anger, and sadness).
- **Motivating oneself:** The ability to (a) channel emotions in the service of a goal, and (b) delay gratification and stifle impulses to obtain a greater goal.
- **Empathy:** The ability to (a) be sensitive to the feelings and concerns of others, (b) take the perspective of others, and (c) appreciate the differences in how people feel about things.
- **Handling relationships:** The ability to (a) perceive and understand the emotions in others, and (b) use this perception and understanding to guide one's action in social and interpersonal situations (interpersonal intelligence).

The five domains can all be addressed within a general education curriculum. For example, we can teach students to identify and become more aware of their own emotions and inner worlds (self-awareness). We can teach them to manage their emotions by helping them discover healthy responses to their feelings of anger, anxiety, sadness, or other emotions. We can help students define goals for themselves and to describe the steps necessary to achieve those goals. And we also can help students develop empathy and learn how to handle a variety of types relationships.

Social Dimension

Social skills and conflict resolution skills can both be used to address the social dimension. *Social skills* are purposeful strategies used to successfully interact with others in interpersonal and social situations. It cannot be assumed, at any level, that students know these. Often students may not have the social skills necessary to function well with others or even be aware of the need for such skills. Thus social skills should be taught explicitly at all levels as appropriate.

Social skills instruction usually involves the following types of skills: interaction skills, conversation and communication skills, skills related to building and maintaining friendships, consideration skills, empathy skills, and conflict resolution skills (discussed in the next paragraph). However, in deciding which social skills to teach, it is always best to observe (or ask) students to see what skills are needed. In addition, a context to learn and practice these skills should be provided. This will enhance learning and facilitates transfer to real-life situations. This context could include small group activities, cooperative learning groups, pairs, recess, and even creative dramatics and role-playing.

Conflict resolution skills are a form of social skills that enable students to constructively deal with the conflicts they will encounter in their own lives. Conflicts that sometimes occur between students in schools are normal and can play an important part in their social and emotional development. These situations provide opportunities for students to begin to learn how to manage their differences and resolve disputes. Thus teachers should resist the temptation to jump in and solve conflict problems for students, as this would rob them of the learning experience. Instead students should be taught the skills to deal with conflict. Below are examples of two conflict strategies that can be taught to students.

- **Resolving conflict using the six-step collaboration process.** The following steps can be used to guide students' thinking through each step: First, identify the source of the conflict. Second, each person lists his or her wants and needs related to the conflict. Third, both parties brainstorm a wide variety of ideas for possible solutions. Fourth, identify the three best solutions. Fifth, evaluate each solution on the basis of costs and rewards for each person. And finally, select the solution or combination of solutions that offers the most benefits and the least costs for implementation. Then implement the solution, revise, and refine as necessary.
- **Conflict resolution bridge.** The conflict resolution bridge works best with younger students. A bridge in the form of ten squares is painted on the playground or taped to a school or classroom floor. Each square contains one of the conflict resolution steps. Students with a conflict start on each side of the bridge. They move toward each other with each step. In the first square, each student describes what he or she wants in terms of the conflict. In the second square students describe their feelings. ("When you ___, I feel ___.") In the third square each student restates the position of the other. (This invites students to take the perspective of the other person in the dispute.) In the fourth square students generate ideas for solutions. Finally, students pick an idea in which they both agree, meet in the middle, and shake hands.

RELATIONSHIPS

Essential characteristic #2: Holistic education promotes relationships.

Within this context, there are several types of relationships. This section will focus on two relationships: teacher-student and student-student.

Teacher-Student

Real teaching of any kind starts with a relationship. Without some sort of relationship, one is just an accumulation of knowledge, pedagogical strategies, and behavior management techniques. The teacher-student relationship is enhanced by following elements.

- **Authenticity and congruence.** For relationships to occur, the teacher must first display authenticity and congruence as described in chapter 16. This enables students to see the human being, not simply a teaching persona and set of strategies. Toward this end, teachers might share bits of their lives with students (as appropriate). Teachers might also identify emotional states when appropriate. For example: "Students, right now I am feeling pretty joyful because . . ." As well, for writing activities, teachers might write about and share their ideas and experiences with students. Finally, teachers might join small group discussions as a participant.
- **Listening skills.** Active listening skills enable a person to by fully present and attend to what another person says with honest intent (Johnson, 2017). *Honest intent* means that you sincerely try to understand and respond to what the other person is saying; you are not simply waiting for a quiet spot to jump into the conversation. Active listening skills enhance teachers' ability to relate to students, parents, and colleagues.

  There are five parts to active listening. First is to make eye contact. Look directly at the person. Second, give complete attention and show interest. Show the speaker that you want to know what he or she has to say. Third, be quiet. Let the other person talk. Do not talk about yourself. Fourth, do not give advice. Your job is to listen. If the speaker asks for your opinion, ask the speaker what he or she thinks. And fifth, ask questions. Again, do not give answers or suggestions. Instead ask questions such as:

  > "Why is it that . . .?"
  > "Do you want to . . .?"
  > "Do you think that . . .?"
  > "What would happen if . . .?"
  > "What do you feel when . . .?"
  > "What is it that you'd like to do . . .?"

- **Trust.** Relationships of any kind are based on trust. Holistic educators recognize that students naturally want to learn so they trust them to learn. Thus, not every assignment needs to be graded. Not every unit needs to be tested. Progress can be gently and infrequently monitored. As well, students are encouraged to demonstrate their learning in ways that are not always measurable. Students do not need to be manipulated by grades or other types of rewards.

Student-Student

Holistic educators create the conditions where students are able to develop relationships with other students.

- **Listening skills.** The active listening skills described for the teacher-student relationship should also be taught to students to enhance their ability to relate to other students. These can be introduced, explicitly taught, and practiced at all levels. These skills are especially relevant in the middle school and high school grades as students are grappling with social and interpersonal dimensions.

    For example, once a week Ms. Perez has listening practice in her seventh-grade class. Students are randomly paired. One person is the listener and the other person is the speaker. She might give the speaker a prompt like, "Describe a problem in your life." Or "Tell about an important event in your life." Other days she might simply say, "What do you want to talk about today?" The speaker shares while the other student engages in active listening. After five minutes, the roles are reversed.
- **See and be seen.** One cannot relate to what one cannot see. Spaces should be provided within the class or curriculum for students to see and be seen by other students. This includes sharing journal entries (see Transpersonal or Transcendent Element section), having class meetings, engaging in small group discussions (see the next bullet), and holding listening practice.
- **Cooperative learning.** Cooperative learning is a structured teaching and learning strategy in which small groups of students work together using a variety of learning activities to accomplish a shared goal (Johnson, 2017). Cooperative learning consists of five elements. First, there is a specific, lesson-related learning task to be accomplished in small groups. Second, there is positive interdependence. This means all students must be actively engaged in the completion of the task in order for the group to be successful. Third, there is face-to-face interaction. Fourth, social skills are practiced. Cooperative learning groups provide a perfect venue to use for teaching the social (interpersonal) skills necessary to function in a group. And fifth, there is time for reflection and review. At end of every cooperative learning activity time is set aside for groups to examine their effectiveness in working together and completing the task.
- **Personal and interpersonal problem-solving.** Here, students work in small cooperative groups of three to five to find solutions for common personal and interpersonal problems. The small group format provides a safe environment for students to explore options and alternatives for problems they may face or be experiencing in their own lives. It also provides students with a variety of ideas and perspectives.

- **Social skills.** Teaching social skills provides the tools students need to form relationships.

REAL-WORLD PROBLEMS, INTEGRATION

Essential characteristic #3: Holistic education seeks to incorporate real-life experiences with learning.

John Dewey (1938) recommended that real-life experiences be incorporated into a curriculum, that the classroom should represent and incorporate what is beyond the classroom. In other words, the wall between the classroom and the real world should disappear to the greatest extent possible. This section demonstrates and describes three ways in which real-life experiences can be incorporated within a curriculum.

Experiential Learning

Experiential learning strives to create learning that is based on real-life experiences. Wurdinger (2005) defines *experiential learning* as a process through which learners construct knowledge and skills from direct experience. That is, students first have a primary experience where they are directly involved with a skill or application. The primary experience here would be a problem, application, or skill taken directly from the real world. It could involve an activity in the real world (outside the classroom). This is followed by a secondary experience in which students are involved with related theory and information. In other words, instead of providing background information to enable students to understand the experience or apply the skill, students learn by first having the experience. Background knowledge is then provided to put their learning in a theoretical context. In this sense, experiential learning is much like discovery learning described in chapter 14.

Problem-Based Learning

Problem-based learning connects the curriculum to the real world by (a) inserting real-world problems into a curriculum or (b) using real-world problems as the basis of a curriculum (Johnson, 2017). These real-world problems might be large societal issues that are addressed on the theoretical level such as: "How can we help the homeless?" They might also be local school or community problems such as: "What can be done to enable people to kayak down Wood River?" Finally, real-world problems might include problems that occur on the personal or interpersonal level. These are problems such as: "What can I do when my best friend is inconsiderate?"

Service Learning

Service learning is an experience in which students learn through active participation in an organized service experience that meets a community need (Johnson, 2009). Four components necessary for service learning experiences: preparation, service, reflection, and celebration. Preparation is used to provide students with the background information and skills necessary for the project. Service involves students engaged in some type of meaningful work. Reflection is the act of thinking critically about the experience afterward, and celebration is a concluding activity used to recognize a job well done.

VALUES AND VIEWS

Essential characteristic #4: Holistic education enables learners to critically examine and define their own values and views.

Values Clarification

Values clarification is a pedagogical strategy that can be effectively used to enable students to identify, analyze, and elucidate their values (Johnson, 2009). Values clarification activities involve defining, listing, ranking, or rating things that students' value or find to be of worth. These things could be traits such as honesty, fortitude, or compassion. These things could also be physical things, people, or experiences.

Below are examples of two possible values clarification activities. These should be adopted and adapted to fit the teaching situation and students' developmental level.

1. **Define that which is valued.** Ask students to list or define five to ten things that they value. This could be material things, personal values, personal characteristics, experiences, activities, or people. After sharing their lists in small groups or in a journal, ask students to identify what their valued things might say about them or who they are.
2. **Rank personal values.** Give students a list of personal values such as honesty, compassion, and hard work and ask them to rank them from most important to least. They should then describe their reasons for picking their top two values. This can be done individually or in small group. Small group activities are effective here because they invite conversation. It is in conversation that students must clarify and communicate that which they value as well as hear others' perspectives.

Views

The T-talk discussion strategy enables students to identify and express their views (Johnson, 2017). It also invites students to experience multiple viewpoints. With adaptation it can be used in kindergarten through high school. These are the steps:

1. **Design a dualistic statement that reflects lesson content, assigned reading, a current event, or a common issue.** A dualistic statement is one in which students have to either agree or disagree. For example: *"Schools should have one online day each week."* This is a statement that students can either support or reject.
2. **Have students work in pairs.** Give each pair a sheet of paper with a large letter T on it. This is the T-chart. List the dualistic statement at the top of the T. On one side of the T-chart, have the pair list at least two ideas to support the statement and on the other side, two ideas to refute the statement. Supporting or refuting ideas should be made regardless of what students might actually think. At this stage partners should not know each other's position. This usually takes about five minutes.
3. **Each pair combines with another pair to form a small group.** After sharing their ideas on both sides of the issue, each group member identifies his or her individual position. The group's task then is to try to reach a consensus. This is where most of the discussion occurs. There will be times when a consensus cannot be reached. When this occurs, the group may need to revise the dualistic statement or simply agree to disagree. All members will get a chance to describe their individual ideas later.
4. **At the end of the small group session, one speaker from each small group shares the group's conclusion with the class.** The speaker has one minute to share their group's position along with two reasons to support the group's position. Example: "Our group believes . . . because (a) . . . and (b) . . ."
5. **The topic is opened for class discussion.** To make this a writing activity, students can also describe their individual opinions in a blog, learning log, short paper, or online discussion site.

TRANSPERSONAL OR TRANSCENDENT ELEMENT

Essential characteristic #5: Holistic education recognizes the transpersonal element.

Transpersonal is that which extends or goes beyond individual consciousness. Transpersonal realms are best accessed by movement away from the external world of the senses toward the internal world of the conscious and unconscious. This could include activities like the use of silence, journal writing, and the arts.

Silence

Include and embrace silence. Silence is one way to enable students to embrace transpersonal dimensions. This could include something as simple as taking thirty seconds to two minutes to breathe deeply, calm the mind, and allow the thoughts and images to come. Here silence is used to bring stillness to the mind in order to enhance self-reflection. To extend this, students can move into pairs or small groups and share an idea that came to them.

Writing Activities

Here are some examples of writing activities:

- **Journal writing.** Journal writing is a natural follow-up to silence. Silence can also be used as a prewriting activity by asking, "What are you thinking about today? Take a few minutes, breathe deeply, and try to focus on what thoughts are running through your head."

  The goal of the journal is to provide a place for students to record their thoughts, observations, impressions, or interesting ideas. It is to be a written version of their thinking/contemplation space and thus it should not be graded for spelling, mechanics, or content. Sometimes a teacher might give a specific journal prompt such as, "What kind of things make you happy?" Or, "Describe a time when you were very angry." The best kinds of journal prompts are more general and allow for students to write about what is important in their lives: "What do you want to say today?" Or, "What's going on in your life?" Or, "What are you thinking about?" Or, "What are you feeling? Why are you feeling this way?"
- **Autobiography.** This is a journal writing activity that invites students to capture and preserve moments from their lives. This type of writing enables students to view these individual moments in a greater context. It also provides a vehicle to analyze episodes and understand the related emotions. Finally, analyzing these past episodes can help students understand and navigate current situations and feelings.
- **Sharing.** Sharing their writing with others allows students to see a commonality of experiences and emotions and understand others at a deeper level. This in turn serves to build relationships. It may also have a certain cathartic effect in that it allows students to identify things that may have been harboring in their unconscious, record them, and then share them with others.

- **Power-write.** A power-write is a strategy in which students try to catch as many ideas as quickly as they can in a three-minute period of time (two minutes for younger students). The goal of the power-write is to get students to bypass the logical mind by rapidly free-associating. Students should quickly write the first thing that pops into their mind without thinking or evaluating. A timer should be used here so that students know they are writing for a specific amount of time.

  Students' writing should be very disjointed here. Encourage students to use scribbles, scratch marks, arrows, diagrams, single words, incomplete sentences, and quick impressions. If done correctly, the power-write will help the writer discover a wealth of images and impressions residing in the unconscious. The elements found within the power-write can be used as the basis for future writing or discussion activities.

The Arts

The arts enable one to capture and express ideas that are often beyond the grasp of literal language. What's more, the arts can provide a more accurate and complete depiction of humans interacting with their external and internal worlds. The arts also provide a platform from which to find balance between inner and outer dimensions. The arts are related to one of the self-actualizing tasks described in chapter 17, where one encounters and then expresses emotions, images, and ideas from intrapersonal dimensions. The arts also engage brain regions that traditional academic activities do not (Shi, et al., 2017). For these reasons and others, the arts as a form of creative expression should be included in curriculums for their own sake (Eisner, 1991). This would include music, dance, visual arts (drawing, painting, photography, and sculpture), drama, video and digital art, filmmaking, creative writing, and poetry.

INTEGRATED STUDIES

Essential characteristic #6: Holistic education recognizes the interconnectedness of all things.

Whereas traditional education is separated into parts by subject matter, branches of knowledge, disciplines, fields, units, and classes, holistic learning theory would posit that such separation does not in actuality exist. That is, the imaginary boundaries between these are human constructs. They do not reflect the view of reality put forth by holistic learning theory in which all things are interconnected and exist in relationship to all other things. One way in which this principle of interconnectedness can be applied is in integrated studies.

Levels of Integration

An integrated study is a form of curriculum or study in which students are able to pursue learning without the restrictions imposed by subject boundaries. John Miller (2007) describes three levels of integration. The first level is *multidisciplinary integration*. This is the lowest level of integration. Here the curriculum retains its subject borders but establishes linkages between other subject areas. For example, a social studies curriculum might reference related concepts in science or art.

The second level is *interdisciplinary integration*. Here, two or three subjects might be organized around a specific theme or problem. For example, if the problem were the Wood River kayaking problem described previously, math, science, and social studies could all be used in solving the problem.

The third level is *transdisciplinary integration*. This is the highest level of integration. Here all subjects are integrated around a broad theme. At this level individual subjects become less apparent as the concepts between subjects and concepts become more numerous and complex.

Steps for Integration

With an integrated curriculum students learn more deeply, because the area of study is approached from a multitude of perspectives. Also, an integrated study employs a variety of forms of representation of ideas, and thus honors students' multiple forms of intelligence and the variety of cognitive strengths (Eisner, 1991). Taken to its furthest end, a learning environment could be created without any curriculum borders.

INTELLIGENT ACTS

This chapter provided some examples of how holistic learning theory may manifest or be applied in a classroom setting. This is by no means a complete list of applications. Again, the ultimate goal of holistic education is to provide instruction, experience, and reflective activities that lead to the furtherance of intelligent acts.

Part VI

Algorithmic Views of Teaching and Learning

Chapters 20 and 21 examine what can be described as an algorithmic view of teaching and learning. Topics include lesson planning, the Hunter lesson plan format, and the Danielson Framework.

Chapter Twenty

Planning for Learning

This chapter describes lesson planning from two different perspectives: algorithmic and heuristic.

ALGORITHMS AND HEURISTICS

An *algorithm* is formula for solving problems. Here you follow a step-by-step set of procedures in order to achieve a specific outcome. In other words, by correctly following a prescribed set of steps in the specified order, you will be led to a predefined solution. Algorithms are useful in mathematics and computer science for calculation, data processing, and automatic reasoning.

A *heuristic* is a general set of principles that are flexibly applied as needed to solve a problem or get a preferred result. Applying these principles will not lead you to a specific outcome, but they can be used to achieve a desired outcome.

Heuristic strategies are useful for the types of real-life problems for which there are not always specific answers. These include problems such as, "How can I keep students engaged in my social studies class?" "How can I get my students motivated to read during the summer?" "What can I do to effectively address this academic standard?" These are all classroom problems for which algorithms would not work. In fact, algorithms have very limited uses outside of controlled contexts such as mathematics and computer science. Most of the problems encountered in the real world require a heuristic solution.

An Algorithm Applied to Teaching

Given the limitation of algorithms in real-world settings, it is surprising that an algorithmic solution is often deemed as being appropriate for a common real-world problem related to teaching and learning. This problem is: "What is the best way to teach this lesson?" An algorithmic view of teaching and learning would posit that an algorithm, in the form of a very specific set of step-by-step procedures, uniformly applied to the process of teaching, is the best solution to this common problem. The algorithm here is manifest in the form of a very, specific lesson plan format (see below) or an instructional model.

The teaching algorithm has had slight variations over time with different titles such as programmed instruction, criterion referenced instruction (CRI), conditions of learning, mastery learning, mastery teaching, strategic instruction, learning strategies, direct instruction, explicit direct instruction, supported instruction, and the framework for teaching. All of these teaching algorithms share a common assumption: If the algorithm is followed explicitly, the teacher can be assured that students will learn. From this perspective the solution for any learning problem is simple: Follow the algorithm.

VARIATIONS ON AN ALGORITHMIC THEME

The Madeline Hunter lesson plan format was popular in the late 1970s and 1980s and is still being used today (Hunter, 1982; Hunter, 2004). Hunter's original purpose was to provide a platform that would enable educators to have conversations about effective teaching. However, it quickly moved away from being a conversational platform to becoming a teaching algorithm. Schools and teacher preparation programs began to use the seven elements described in Hunter's model of instruction to observe and evaluate teachers. These seven elements became known as the Hunter Lesson Plan. They are described below:

1. **Anticipatory set.** The teacher introduces students to the lesson. It is used to grab students' attention, stimulate curiosity, or get them ready for learning.
2. **Purpose.** The teacher explains the purpose of the lesson to students. This is also used to provide an overview of what is to be learned. Often teachers describe what students should be able to do after the lesson.
3. **Input and modeling.** The teacher provides the information that students need to know to understand the lesson concept or skill. The teacher demonstrates what is to be learned.

4. **Check for understanding.** The teacher checks to see if students understand what was presented in the input. This is called formative assessment. Questions are often used here as a probe to check for understanding.
5. **Guided practice.** The teacher leads students through a highly structured activity that enables them to practice their new learning with the guidance and support of the teacher.
6. **Independent practice.** Students are released to practice their learning on their own. This is often homework or seatwork assignments given to practice the material or skill without teacher supervision.
7. **Closure.** Here the teacher brings the lesson to some kind of conclusion. The teacher might review the major ideas, use a graphic organizer to organize content, reinforce important concepts, or ask some clarifying questions. The closure should help bring things together in students' minds.

Limitations of a Teaching Algorithm

If used as a general guide or scaffold, the Hunter Lesson Plan format might be helpful for beginning teachers if it is flexibly applied and used in limited situations. However, once it becomes an algorithm it tends to inhibit more than enhance good teaching. Some of the limitations include the following:

1. The Hunter Lesson Plan involves a form of direct instruction. While direct instruction is effective for learning low-level facts and skills, it is not very effective for higher level learning (Eppley and Dudley-Marling, 2018).
2. While there is research to support the idea that planning enhances teacher effectiveness and student learning (Freiberg and Driscoll, 1992; Stringfield and Teddlie, 1991; Walberg, 1991); little evidence can be found to support one type of lesson plan format over another. That is, there is little if any research comparing the Hunter model to more heuristic lesson planning formats.
3. The Hunter Lesson Plan leads to the false assumption that there is a standardized teaching process. Trying to standardize the teaching process does not enable individual teachers to utilize their unique strengths. Neither does it recognize the diversity of learners with a wide range of abilities, interests, and learning styles.
4. While individual elements of this format might be necessary in certain teaching situations, all the elements are not necessary in every lesson. That is, effective learning experiences can be created without many of these elements, and ineffective learning experiences can occur despite the inclusion of all of these elements.

TWO BASIC LESSON PLAN FORMATS

Teaching is a complex endeavor. It is made infinitely more so by external demands that would have teachers try to shoehorn their lesson plans to fit into an overly cumbersome, standardized lesson plan format. Also, there is no singular type of lesson plan that works best for all situations. Instead, different kinds of lessons call for different kinds of lesson plan formats (Johnson, 2017). And if teachers understand some of the basic principles of human learning described in this book, the overly complex teaching recipes or cumbersome lesson formats do not need to be used. Described here are two basic lesson plan forms: a schema-building lesson plan and a skills lesson plan. These are heuristic solutions to the problem of planning effective lessons.

A Basic Schema-Building Lesson

The schema-building lesson plan is designed to enable the assimilation and accommodation of information into students' existing and developing schemata. The three basic elements necessary to design this type of lesson are (a) a purpose statement, (b) input, and (c) an activity.

1. **Purpose statement.** In designing a learning experience, you should begin with a specific idea of what it is you wish to teach. A purpose statement is used here. This is a single statement identifying what you want students to learn or know. Behavioral terms or a behavioral objective are not used because true learning cannot be observed (explained later in this chapter). The following is an example of a purpose statement: *Students will learn about amphibians.* Everything that follows the purpose statement in a lesson plan (input and activities) should support it. Anything that does not support the purpose statement should be not be included in the lesson.
2. **Input.** Input is the heart of the schema-building lesson plan. Here you present the specific information that students need in order to meet the lesson purpose. Any discussion questions used as part of the lesson should also be included here. This should be presented in an organized fashion using language and terms that students will understand. It is recommended that your plan use list form or outline form with short, abbreviated sentences. This will allow you to quickly see the structure and sequence of the lesson as you are planning it. This will also enable you to teach from the lesson plan without reading directly from it.
3. **Independent practice.** Independent practice is an activity that enables students to manipulate or interact with the information provided in the

input. This could include activities for students to practice their learning, extend their learning, or apply things they have learned.

A Basic Skills Lesson Plan

Teaching a skill of any kind incorporates four components that are incorporated into a slightly different lesson plan form: (a) purpose statement, (b) direct instruction and modeling, (c) guided practice, and (d) independent practice (Johnson, 2000).

1. **Purpose Statement.** This is a one-sentence statement that identifies the skill that you want students to learn about or be able to do.
2. **Input.** The input is used to tell students exactly what they need to know in order to perform the skill. Here you provide explicit instruction related to how the skill might be used and the specific steps for doing the skill. You should also demonstrate and model it by thinking aloud while going through each step.
3. **Guided practice.** Guided practice, sometimes referred to as scaffolded instruction, is at the heart of teaching a skill of any kind (Rosenshine, 2012). The goal here is to provide the support necessary for students to use the skill independently. Here you take all students through each step of the skill several times, each time providing less scaffolding (see chapter 9).
4. **Independent practice.** This is an activity designed to enable students to independently practice or reinforce the skill they have just learned. This may include an in-class activity or homework. If the skills lesson has been taught effectively, students should be able to complete this with a 95 to 100 percent success ratio (Brophy, 1986).

Regular practice, review, and integration. This element is not part of the skills lesson plan; however, it should be understood that mastery of any skill never occurs with a single lesson or exposure. When learning any kind of skill, students need to revisit and review it many times for it to become part of their repertoire. Regular practice allows for efficiency and automaticity.

OBJECTIVES AND ASSESSMENT

Two final areas to consider when planning for instruction are behavioral objectives and assessment.

Behavioral Objectives and Purpose Statements

Behavioral learning theory describes learning as a change in behavior that occurs as a result of instruction or experience. Behavioral objectives are in alignment with this theory (see chapter 6). A behavioral objective is a single-sentence statement describing the desired outcome for the lesson in terms of a specific behavior. In other words, if the lesson were successful, you would expect to see that behavior.

Neurological, cognitive, and transformative learning theories all describe learning as an internal event. It is a change in neural pathways, cognitive structures, or consciousness. From these perspectives learning cannot be directly observed; hence, a behavioral objective would not be appropriate. Instead, from these theoretical perspectives, a purpose statement is appropriate.

To compare behavioral objectives and purpose statements, examples of both are included here:

Behavioral objective: Students will correctly identify and describe the essential elements of classical conditioning.

Purpose statement: Students will learn about classical conditioning.

Behavioral objective: Students will create a time line to show seven important events in the origin of Blue Earth County.

Purpose statement: Students will learn about the origin of Blue Earth County.

Behavioral objective: Students will demonstrate their knowledge of amphibians by successfully completing the amphibian worksheet.

Purpose statement: Students will learn about amphibians.

Behavioral objective: Students will be able to correctly identify the verbs used in their daily writing sample.

Purpose statement: Students will learn about verbs.

Limitations of Behavioral Objectives

Below are four reasons to support the use of purpose statements over behavioral objectives:

1. **Real learning is not defined by or confined to a behavioral objective**. Deep, meaningful learning often goes far beyond the behavioral objective. If you define what must be, you run the risk of limiting what

might be. Thus behavioral objectives can stymie rather than enhance real learning.

2. **Learning is not uniform.** A major tenet of many of the learning theories described in this book is that we construct new knowledge based on our current knowledge. Thus, during any given lesson, each learner is constructing a slightly different view of the new concept or topic based on his or her background knowledge. To assume uniformity limits learning. Thus, while we provide the same input, the levels and types of learning are going to be a bit different for each student. In other words, each student will take something different from the lesson.

3. **Behavioral objectives focus on standardization.** Humans are not standardized entities. In any normal population, scores will be distributed along a bell-shaped curve. If the same behavioral objective, input, and assignment are used for all students in an average classroom, 68 percent of the students might be adequately challenged. However, 16 percent will be overchallenged, feel frustrated, and will fail. Another 16 percent will be underchallenged and feel frustrated and bored.

4. **Behavioral objectives promote the fallacy of mastery.** Learning is never complete with a single encounter with any skill or concept. We need to retouch, revisit, and review concepts and skills many times at successively higher levels in a variety of contexts for mastery to occur.

Assessment Is Optional

Many approaches to lesson planning require a plan for assessment. This is a description of how you will determine if the behavioral objective or purpose statement has been met. However, teaching is always more effective if the focus is on students' learning rather than the assessment of learning. Thus, not every lesson should include a plan for assessment.

If you do not include a plan for assessment, how do you know if learning has occurred? A more appropriate question to ask is, "How do you know if teaching has occurred?" In other words, if the focus is on effective teaching using strategies that are aligned with research-based theory, most of the learning will take care of itself.

While it is not appropriate to include a plan for assessment with every lesson, there are times and places when it is appropriate to assess and describe students' learning. Remember: Learning is seldom complete after a single encounter with any skill or concept. Instead, students need to review, reengage, reflect, practice, and apply new skills and concepts before they are fully learned.

Therefore a more effective approach to assessment is to collect small bits of meaningful data at specific places in the curriculum to see if and to what degree learning is taking place. In this way assessment is very much like collecting soils samples: You do not dig up the entire lawn to see what kind of soil you have. Instead you take small samples from different parts of the lawn.

Reflection

Reflection is not a formal part of a lesson plan, but it is a critical element in being and becoming a master teacher (Noormohammid, 2014; Zeichner and Liston, 2014). As such, it is an essential part of any lesson. Reflection occurs during the teaching episode in what is called "formative assessment." It also occurs after the teaching episode in what is called "summative assessment." Reflective thinking occurs on three levels.

- **Level 1: Teaching effectiveness.** Effective teachers reflect to assess learning outcomes (Sadker, Sadker and Zittleman, 2008). They examine the teaching episode in order to identify those things that worked well and those things that could have been done differently.
- **Level 2: Research, research-based practices, or research-based theories.** Decisions made by expert teachers are grounded in established theory and research-based practices (Porter, Youngs and Odden, 2001; Stanovich and Stanovich, 2003). Effective teachers pause to examine their teaching practice to see if what they are doing aligns with a body of research and research-based theories related to teaching and learning. Of course it is hard to reflect at this level if you have nothing upon which to reflect. Thus you can see the importance of having sufficient knowledge in each of the four areas described in chapter 1.
- **Level 3: Values and philosophy.** Teaching at the highest level requires that teachers pause to consider if what they are doing is in harmony with their personal and professional values and their philosophy (Dewey, 1934).

INTERNALIZATION

If you are a beginning teacher, know that whatever lesson plan format you are currently using will look much different than the format you will eventually use after a few years of experience. This is because you have internalized the structure. This is the Vygotskian idea that thinking moves from outside to in.

Chapter Twenty-One

The Danielson Framework

SEVENTY-SIX TINY ELEMENTS

Like the Hunter Lesson Plan described in chapter 20, the Danielson Framework has also been converted into a teaching algorithm and used to evaluate teachers.

A Conversation Stopper

The Danielson Framework (1996) has been around for over twenty years. It is still being used in various forms in many schools and teacher-preparation programs. Charlotte Danielson attempted to deconstruct what she perceived as professional teaching practice by breaking it down into four domains: (1) planning and preparation, (2) classroom environment, (3) instruction, and (4) professional responsibilities. These four domains were then broken into twenty-two components and then into seventy-six tiny elements. Danielson included a rubric for each of the seventy-six elements, which described four levels of teacher performance: unsatisfactory, basic, proficient, and distinguished levels.

In designing this framework, Danielson defined what she considered to be effective teaching and then selected elements that she decided were important for being and becoming a professional educator. Like Madeline Hunter, her goal initially was to use the framework to create conversations about the elements of good teaching. In reviewing the seventy-six tiny elements, there are indeed many that can contribute to important educational conversations. (There are also some elements that are highly subjective with supporting research that is, at best, peripheral.)

However, conversation implies a two-way flow of ideas. When rubrics are created and levels of performance are described, there is little, if any, room for conversation. What is created instead is an evaluation tool, variations of which are being used today in teacher-preparation programs and public schools in an attempt to create a certain type of teacher with a set of values and teaching philosophy that somebody other than the teacher being evaluated has determined to be appropriate.

A Subjective Examination of Research

Although the framework might be perceived by some to be an objective examination and application of empirical research, Danielson's description of professional practice is highly subjective in terms of the elements that were selected for consideration and the limited depth and breadth of research that was examined. This resulted in a fairly narrow, theoretical perspective related to teaching.

If instead a more expansive set of data were examined from a wider variety of fields related to human learning, and if a more inclusive lens were used to interpret this data, it is highly likely that a much different set of domains, components, and elements would be included. It is doubtful that the state of being and becoming an effective educator would be reduced to seventy-six elements. It is doubtful as well that these seventy-six elements would be put on a four-point scale and used to evaluate teachers.

Danielson claims that her framework is research-based (Danielson, 2007); however, just like Madeline Hunter's lesson plan, this is also a bit misleading. While research can be found to support many (but not all) of Danielson's seventy-six elements, putting these elements together in a single framework does not mean that the framework itself is supported by research. It just means that it is a list of seventy-six elements, some of which are supported by research and some of which are not.

There is no comparative research suggesting that the Danielson Framework is any more effective for enhancing the professional practice of preservice and practicing teachers than other frameworks, checklists, rubrics, models, sets of dispositions, standards, assessment devices, professional development strategies, or reflective practices. There is no research to support the idea that using these seventy-six tiny elements is a more effective means of teacher assessment and evaluation than other methods.

In addition, there should be no doubt that the current unstated purpose of the Danielson Framework is to enable the educational industrial complex to generate greater profits (Brightman and Gutmore, 2002). If instead the purpose of the framework was to actually improve education, a set of domains and components would be included for principals and administrators, school-board members, legislators, professors at teacher-preparation institutions, scholars, and anybody else making decisions or recommendations about schools and classrooms.

Such domains, uniformly applied, would invite all to begin to explore a wider range of research and ideas related to education and human learning. This type of application would have the potential to evolve our current educational system and be of benefit to those other than a few financial stakeholders. However, since the framework was introduced in 1996, additional domains and components have not been included.

Creating Another Teaching Algorithm

The Danielson Framework also has been used to design new teaching algorithms based on her Instruction Plan for a Single Lesson. Whereas Madeline Hunter included seven elements, teachers using this lesson plan format are asked to include and describe ten elements when preparing a lesson:

1. Goals for the lesson
2. Importance of lesson goals
3. Relationship of lesson goals to:

   a. content standards: CCSS or state standards
   b. broader curriculum goals

4. Plan for student engagement

   a. teacher strategies
   b. student activities
   c. approximate time

5. Description of students with special needs
6. Common student difficulties

   a. common difficulties
   b. how they will be addressed

7. Students with special needs

   a. struggling learners
   b. gifted learners
   c. others

8. Materials and other resources
9. Plan for assessment

   a. goals and criteria

    b. assessment procedures

    c. tests, performances, rubrics, or checklists that are used

10. Plan for using assessment data

This new teaching algorithm is even more cumbersome than Hunter's lesson plant format.

BEING AND BECOMING A MASTER TEACHER

You cannot deconstruct the complex process of being and becoming a master teacher into seventy-six tiny elements and expect to create a finished teaching product by putting all the pieces back together again. This Humpty Dumpty approach is what Danielson has tried to do with her framework.

Instead, being and becoming a master teacher occurs over time and involves four components: knowing, planning, doing, and reflecting.

- **Knowing.** Teachers need to have an organized body of knowledge related to teaching and learning (Darling-Hammond, 1999; Sternberg and Williams, 2010). This organized body of knowledge enables teachers to align the approaches and strategies they use with a body of research and to make decisions that are more likely to enhance their students' learning. As stated in chapter 1, there are four areas of knowledge that are necessary to become an expert teacher (Eggen and Kauchak, 2007): (a) content knowledge, (b) pedagogical knowledge, (c) pedagogical content knowledge, and (d) knowledge of learners and the learning process.
- **Planning.** Good teaching does not happen by accident. Effective teachers plan their learning experiences (Hay/McBer, 2000). They decide exactly what they want students to learn, the teaching strategies they will use, the questions they may ask students, and related activities and assignments. In your classrooms, planning will enable you to create more purposeful and effective instruction and results with fewer behavior management issues.
- **Doing.** This third element is where you actually teach the lesson. Here you present the material to be learned using a variety of research-based methodologies and teaching strategies (Johnson, 2017). However, the first two elements (knowing and planning) need to be addressed before you can function well here
- **Reflecting.** What separates effective teachers from ineffective teachers is the propensity to reflect (Zeichner and Liston, 2014). Being an effective teacher does not mean that you do not make mistakes or have bad lessons. (If you never make mistakes it probably means that you have not experimented or tried enough new things.) The difference is that effective teach-

ers think about those mistakes and bad lessons so that they can figure out what went wrong and how they might change the lesson. Ineffective teachers do not do this.

Chapter Twenty-Two

Defining Teaching

THREE VIEWS OF TEACHING

There are three common views or conceptions of teaching: teaching as transmission, teaching as transaction, and teaching as transformation (Miller, 1996).

Teaching as Transmission

From this perspective, teaching is the act of transmitting knowledge from Point A (teacher's head) to Point B (students' heads). This is a teacher-centered approach in which the teacher is the dispenser of knowledge, the arbitrator of truth, and the final evaluator of learning. A teacher's job from this perspective is to supply students with a designated body of knowledge or set of skills in a predetermined order. Academic achievement is seen as the students' ability to demonstrate, replicate, or retransmit this designated body of knowledge or set of skills back to the teacher or to some other measuring agency or entity. From this perspective standardized tests are considered to be an apt measure of students' learning.

Five essential constructs related to this view are as follows:

- **Learning:** A relatively permanent change in behavior (or behavioral potentiality) that occurs as a result of experience
- **Role of teacher:** Supply students with designated body of knowledge or set of skills
- **Role of student:** Passively receive information or replicate skills
- **Guiding philosophy:** Positivism
- **Theoretical basis:** Behaviorism and behavioral learning theories

Teaching as Transaction

From this perspective, teaching is the process of creating situations whereby students are able to interact with the material to be learned in order to construct knowledge. Constructivism is an educational philosophy consistent with this view. Here, knowledge is not passively received; instead it is actively built up or constructed by students as they connect their past knowledge and experiences with new information (Santrock, 2004). And just as each student's past knowledge and experiences are different, so too are the interpretation, understanding, and meaning of the new information that each ultimately constructs.

Teachers are not expected to pour knowledge into the heads of students. Instead they assist them in their construction of knowledge and development of skills by creating experiences where students can use their current understanding of knowledge and skills to learn new knowledge and skills. Academic achievement from this perspective is seen as the students' ability to use this knowledge and skills to solve real-world problems or to create products or performances that are valued in one or more cultural settings.

Five essential constructs related to this view are as follows:

- **Learning:** A change in cognitive structures or neural networks that occurs as a result of instruction or experience
- **Role of teacher:** Help students transact with knowledge to create personal meaning
- **Role of student:** Interact with information, construct knowledge
- **Guiding philosophy:** Constructivism
- **Theoretical basis:** Cognitive psychology, cognitive learning theories, neuroscience, and neurological learning theories

Teaching as Transformation

From this perspective, teaching is creating conditions that have the potential to transform the learner on many different levels (cognitive, emotional, social, intuitive, creative, transpersonal, and others). Transformational teaching invites both students and teachers to discover their full potential as learners and teachers, as members of society, and as human beings. The ultimate transformational goal is to help develop more nurturing human beings who are better able to perceive the interconnectedness of all human, plant, and animal life (Narve, 2001).

Learning is said to have occurred when educational experiences elicit a transformation of consciousness that leads to a greater understanding of and care for self, others, and the environment. Academic achievement from this perspective is similar to self-actualization. That is, it is perceived as discovering and developing each individual's unique talents and capabilities to the fullest extent possible. Academic achievement also involves becoming aware of the multiple dimensions of self and expanding one's consciousness.

Five essential constructs related to this view are as follows:

- **Learning:** Movement toward self-actualization that occurs as a result of instruction experience, or a change of consciousness that leads to a greater understanding of and care for self, others, and one's environment
- **Role of teacher:** Create transforming conditions and experiences, enable students to perceive connections, and encourage inner exploration
- **Role of student:** Use information and experiences for self-transformation; reflect and search for meaning; discover and develop talents
- **Guiding philosophy:** Holism
- **Theoretical basis:** Transpersonal psychology and transformational learning theories

Chapter Twenty-Three

Defining Your Educational Philosophy

In reading this book, you encountered a variety of theories. Hopefully you have chosen elements of each that have resonated with you. Now you are ready to examine your educational philosophy.

A *philosophy* is a set of principles based on one's values and beliefs that are used to guide one's behavior. Even though your educational philosophy may not be clearly defined, it is the basis for everything you do as a teacher (DeCarvalho, 1991). It guides your decision-making, influences how you perceive and understand new information, and determines your goals and beliefs (Gutek, 2004). An educational philosophy outlines what you believe to be the purpose of education, the role of the student in education, and the role of the teacher.

Educational philosophies address the following kinds of questions: Why do we educate people? How should we educate people? How does education affect society? How does education affect humanity? Who benefits from a particular type of education? What ethical guidelines should be used? What traits should be valued? Why type of thinking is of worth? How should we come to know the world and make decisions? What is the educational ideal? What is the nature of reality? What do we believe to be true regarding knowledge and truth? How do we come to know? What do you believe to be true regarding humans and human learning?

ELEMENTS OF AN EDUCATIONAL PHILOSOPHY

If you do an Internet search using the terms *educational philosophy* or *teaching philosophy*, you will see that they come in a variety of forms. There are common but not universal elements included in an educational or teaching philosophy. For this chapter, we will focus on four elements. However, to be of use, your educational philosophy will need to be designed so that you can use it to guide and direct your thinking and teaching practice. Therefore, it is recommended that you add additional elements or adopt the ones here to suit your purpose.

- **The purpose of education.** Why do schools exist in our society? What purpose do these serve? Why do our societies invest so much time and resources on educating developing humans? To what end? How does this benefit the society or group?
- **Goals.** Based on your defined purpose, what are some short- or long-term goals?
- **Principles.** Based on your values, what are some guiding principles or things you believe to be true regarding education, teaching, or learning? Here you should prepare a set of propositions that will serve as a foundation for your beliefs or actions.
- **Action statements.** Based on your philosophy, goals, beliefs, and values, what are some action statements? What will you do or strive to do in your classroom? What might we see if we come into your classroom? What do you aspire to do or accomplish? What are some processes and practices you will adopt?

THE NATURE OF EDUCATIONAL PHILOSOPHIES

Defining and elucidating your educational philosophy will enhance your ability to align it with your teaching practice. However, there are four things to note about educational philosophies:

1. **They evolve.** Educational philosophies evolve and change over time as a result of experience, interactions with others, reflection, and new knowledge and experiences. This is good. If you believe the same things in the same sorts of ways that you did five or ten years ago, you have not grown. Even with the most strongly held beliefs, you may still believe them, but you believe more about them, you believe them at different levels, or you believe them in different ways if you are continuing to grow. If you are learning and evolving, your educational philosophy will continue to grow and evolve throughout your career.
2. **You must develop your own.** To be of any use, your philosophy must be aligned with your values and beliefs. (This is why it is important to identify what you value and believe.) There is no such thing as the "correct" philosophy. Effective teachers and people of good character often have differing educational philosophies. This also is a good thing as it leads to continued reflection, dialogue, and refinement. And

whether it be a political philosophy, religious philosophy, or educational philosophy, forcing one's philosophy on another is the ultimate form of domination and control. These are not traits to which we aspire in a democratic society.

3. **Philosophical differences can strengthen a school.** Differing educational philosophies within an educational setting is not a sign of dysfunction. Philosophical differences can strengthen a school. As long as colleagues listen and respect philosophical differences, differences can provide a variety of perspectives on curriculum, school issues, and other learning experiences.

4. **Educational philosophies should be like a lesson purpose statement.** Everything that follows a purpose statement should be to support or reach that objective. In the same way, everything that follows your educational philosophy should support or be in alignment with your philosophy. To the greatest extent possible, your teaching practices should align with your philosophy. This enables you to teach from your authentic self. When teaching from here, teaching seems effortless and is always effective.

INTEGRATION

To teach from your philosophy is to teach with integrity. There is an integration of your personal core values and beliefs with your professional thoughts and actions. If you teach from your philosophy, you will never be wrong. At this point you should be ready to begin to define and describe your educational philosophy. Remember: A philosophy is a guiding set of principles based on your values and beliefs.

References

Aikens, N., Klein, A. K., Tarullo, L., and West, J., (2013). Getting Ready for Kindergarten: Children's Progress During Head Start. *FACES 2009 Report. OPRE Report 2013–21a.* Washington, DC: Office of Planning, Research and Evaluation, Administration for Children and Families, US Department of Health and Human Services.

Al-Khalili, J. (1999). *Black holes, worm holes and time machines.* London: Institute of Physics Publishing.

Alleman, J., Brophy, J., Knighton, B., Ley, B., Botwinski, B., and Middlestead, S., (2010). *Homework done right: Powerful learning in real-life situations.* New York: Skyhorse Publishing.

Allington, R. L. (2006). *What really matters for struggling readers: Designing research-based programs* (2nd ed.). Boston, MA: Allyn and Bacon.

Ausubel, D. P. (1960). The use of advance organizers in the learning and retention of meaningful verbal material. *Journal of educational psychology, 51*, 267–272.

Ausubel, D. P. (1977). The facilitation of meaningful verbal learning in the classroom. *Educational psychologist, 12,* 162–178.

Ausubel, D., Novak, J., and Hanesian, H. (1978). *Educational Psychology: A Cognitive View* (2nd ed.). New York: Holt, Rinehart and Winston.

Ausubel, D. P. and Robinson, F. G. (1969). *School learning: An introduction to educational psychology.* New York: Holt, Rinehart and Winston.

Bura, A. Ross, D., and Ross, S. A (1961). Transmission of aggression through the imitation of aggressive models. *Journal of Abnormal and Social Psychology , 63,* 575–582.

Beck, S. W. (2017). Educational innovation as re-mediation: A sociocultural perspective. *English teaching: Practice and critique, 16,* 29–39.

Bloom, B. S. (1956). *Taxonomy of educational objectives, Handbook I; The cognitive domain.* New York: David McKay.

Bozkurt, G. (2017). Social constructivism: Does it succeed in reconciling individual cognition with social teaching and learning practices in mathematics? *Journal of Education and Practice, 8,* 210–218.

Brightman, H. J. and Gutmore, G. (2002) The Educational-Industrial Complex. *The Educational Forum, 66 (4),* 302–308, DOI:10.1080/00131720208984848.

Brophy, J. (1986). Teacher influences on student achievement. *American Psychologist, 41,* 1069–1077.

Bruer, J. T. (1999). *Schools for thought: A science of learning in the classroom.* Cambridge, MA: MIT Press.

Bruner, J. (1966). *Toward the theory of instruction.* Cambridge, MA: Harvard University Press

Bruner, J. (1977). *The process of education.* Cambridge, MA: Harvard University Press.

Campbell, J. (1968). *The hero with a thousand faces* (2nd ed.). Princeton, NJ: Princeton University Press.

Chase, W. G., and Simon, H. A. (1973). The mind's eye in chess. In W. G. Chase, (Ed.), *Visual information processing*, 215–281. New York: Academic Press.

Clark, E. T. (1991). Holistic education: A search for wholeness. In R. Miller (Ed.), *In New Directions in Education*, 53–62. Brandon, VT: Holistic Education Press.

Combs, A. (1999). *Being and becoming: A field approach to psychology.* New York: Springer Publishing Company.

Craik, F. I. M. and Lockhart, R. S. (1972). Levels of processing: A framework for memory research. *Journal of Verbal Learning and Verbal Behavior, 11,* 671–684.

Counsel for Secular Humanism. Definition of secular humanism. www.secularhumanism.org, retrieved June 12, 2006.

Danielson, C. (1996). *Enhancing professional practice: A framework for teaching.* Alexandra, VA: Association for Supervision and Curriculum Development.

Danielson, C. (2007). *Enhancing professional practice: A framework for teaching.* Alexandria, VA: Association for Supervision and Curriculum Development.

Darling-Hammond, L. (1999). *Teacher quality and study achievement: A review of state policy evidence.* Seattle, WA: Center for the Study of Teaching and Policy, University of Washington.

DeCarvalho, R. (1991). The humanistic paradigm in education. *The Humanistic Psychologist, 19*(1), 88–104

Dewey, J. (1938). *Experience and education.* New York: Touchstone.

Doyle, T. and Zakrajsek, T. D. (2013) *The new science of learning: How to learn in harmony with your brain* . Sterling, VA: Stylus Publishing, LLC.

Eggen, P. and Kauchak, D. (2007). *Educational psychology: Windows on classrooms.* Upper Saddle River, NJ: Pearson.

Eggen, P. and Kauchak, D. (2020). *Using educational psychology in teaching* (11th ed.). Hoboken, NJ: Pearson

Eisner, E. (1991). Art, music, and literature. In J. Shaver (Ed.), *Handbook of research on social studies teaching and learning.* New York: Macmillan.

Eppley, K. and Dudley-Marling, C. (2018). Does direction instruction work?: A critical assessment of direct instruction research and its theoretical perspective. *Journal of Curriculum and Pedagogy, 14,* 1–20.

Freiberg, H. J. and Driscoll, A. (1992). *Universal teaching strategies.* Needham Heights, MA: Allyn and Bacon.

Gerrig, R. J. and Zimbardo, P. G. (2008). *Psychology and life* (18th ed). Boston, MA; Pearson Education.

Goldstein, E. B. (2008). *Cognitive psychology* (2nd ed.) Belmont, CA: Thomson Higher Education.

Goleman, D. (1995). *Emotional intelligence.* New York: Bantam Books.

Goodman, K. S., Fries, P. H., and Strauss, S. L. (2016). *Reading the grand illusion: How and why people make sense of print.* New York: Routledge.

Goswami, A., Reed, R., and Goswami, M. (1993). *The self-aware universe: How consciousness creates the material world.* New York: Putnam Books.

Gutek, G. (2004). *Philosophical and ideological voices in education.* Boston, MA: Pearson Education, Inc.

Hanh, T. (1998). *The heart of the Buddha's teaching: Transforming suffering into peace, joy and liberation.* Berkeley, CA: Parallax Press.

Hattie, J. (2012). *Visible learning for teachers: Maximizing impact on learning.* New York: Routledge.

Hattie, J. and Yates, G. (2014). *Visible learning and the science of how we learn.* New York: Routledge.

Hawkins, J. (2004). *On intelligence.* New York: Times Books.

Hergenhahn, B. R. and Olson, M. H. (2005). *An introduction to theories of learning* (7th ed.). Upper Saddle River, NJ: Pearson/Prentice Hall.

Hay/McBer (2000). Research into teacher effectiveness: A model of teacher effectiveness report by Hay/McBer to the Department for Education and Employment. Report prepared by Hay/McBer for the government of the United Kingdom, available at http://www.dfee.gov. uk/teachingreforms/mcber/.

Johnson, A. (2000). *Up and out: Using creative and critical thinking skills to enhance learning.* Boston: Allyn and Bacon.

Johnson, A. (2009). *Making connections in elementary and middle school social studies* (2nd ed.). Thousand Oaks, CA: SAGE Publications.

Johnson, A. (2013). *Educational psychology: Theories of learning and human development.* El Cajon, CA: National Social Science Press.

Johnson, A. (2016). *10 essential instructional elements for students with reading difficulties: A brain-friendly approach.* Thousand Oaks, CA: Corwin

Johnson, A. (2017). *Teaching strategies for all teachers.* Lanham, MD: Rowman and Little-field.

Jones, K. (1999). Jungian theory. In M. Runco and S. Pritzker (Eds.). *Encyclopedia of creativity* (vol 2). New York: Academic Press.

Jung, C. G. (1938). *Psychology and religion.* New Haven, CT: Yale University Press.

Lattal, K. (1998). A century of effect: Legacies of E. L. Thorndike's animal intelligence monograph. *Journal of The Experimental Analysis of Behavior, 70,* 325–336.

LeFrancois, G. R. (2006). *Theories of learning* (5th ed.). Belmont, CA: Thompson/Wadsworth.

LeFrancois, G. R. (2011). *Theories of human learning: What the professor said* (6th ed.). Belmont, CA: Thomson Wadsworth.

Lim, J., Reiser, R., and Z. Olina. (2009) The effects of part-task and whole-task instructional approaches on acquisition and transfer of a complex cognitive skill. *Educational Technology Research and Development, 57,* 61–77.

Maslow, A. (1968). *Toward a psychology of being* (3rd ed.). New York. John Wiley and Sons, Inc.

Miller, J. P. (1996). *The Holistic Curriculum.* Toronto: OISE Press.

Miller, J. P. (2000). *Education and the soul: Toward a spiritual curriculum.* Albany: State University of New York Press, Albany.

Miller, J. P. (2007). *The holistic curriculum (2nd ed.).* Toronto, Ont. Canada: OISE Press.

Morris, J. (1978). Psychology and teaching: A humanistic view. New York: Random House

Nakagawa, Y. (2002). Education for awakening: An eastern approach to holistic education. Toronto, Ontario: OISE Press, Inc.

National Research Council (2000). *How people learn: Brain, mind, experience, and school.* J. Bransford, A. Brown, R. Cocking (Eds.). Washington, DC: National Academy Press.

Narve, R. G. (2001). *Holistic education: Pedagogy of universal love.* Brandon, VT: Foundation for Educational Renewal.

Noormohammadi, S. (2014). "Teacher reflection and its relation to teach efficacy and autonomy" (2014). *Procedia–Social and Behavioral Sciences, 98* (6), 1380–1389.

Olson, M. H. and Hergenhahn, B. R. (2009). *An introduction to theories of learning* (8th ed.). Upper Saddle, NJ: Pearson.

Ormrod, J. E. (2012). *Human learning* (6th ed). Boston, MA: Pearson

Ormrod, J. E., Anderman, E. M., and Anderman, L. (2020). *Educational psychology: Developing learners.* Hoboken, NJ: Pearson.

Palmer, P. J. (1993). *To know as we are know: Education as a spiritual journey.* San Francisco, CA: HarperSanFrancisco.

Patteron, C. H. (1987). What has happened to humanistic education? *Michigan Journal for Counseling and Development, 18,* 9–10.

Patterson, C. H. (1973). *Humanistic education.* Englewood Cliffs, NJ: Prentice-Hall.

Paulson, E. J., and Goodman, K. S. (2008). Re-reading eye-movement research: Support for transactional models of reading, 25–50. In A. Flurky, E. Paulson and K Goodman (Eds.) *Scientific Realism in Studies of Reading,* New York: LEA.

Pearson, C. S. (1989). *The hero within: Six archetypes we live by.* New York: HarperCollins.

Perkins, D. N. and Salomon, G. (2012). Knowledge to go: A motivational and dispositional view of transfer. *Educational Psychologist, 47 (3),* 248–258.

Pfeiffer, S. (2000). Emotional intelligence: Popular but elusive construct. *Roeper Review, 23,* 138–142.

Purves, D., Brannon, E., Cabeza, R., Huettel, S., LaBar, K., Plat, M., and Woldorff, M. (2012). *Principles of Cognitive Neuroscience* (2nd ed). Sunderland, MA: Sinauer Associates, Inc.

Rayner, K., Liversedge, S. P., White, S. J., and Vergilino-Perez, D. (2003). Reading disappearing text: Cognitive control of eye movements. *Psychological Science, 14,* 385–388.

Revlin, R. (2013). *Cognition: Theory and practice.* New York: Worth Publishers.

Rogers, C. R. (1961). *On becoming a person.* Boston: Houghton Mifflin Company.

Rogers, C. R. (1969). *Freedom to learn.* Columbus, OH: Merrill Publishing Company.

Rogers, C. R. and Freiberg, H. J. (1994). *Freedom to learn* (3rd ed.). Columbus, OH: Merrill/Macmillan.

Rosenshine, B. (2012). Principles of instruction: Research-based strategies that all teachers should know. *American Educator, 36,* 12–9.

Russel-Chapin, L. A., Rybak, C. J., and Copilevitz, T. B. (1996). The art of teaching Jungian analysis. *Journal of Humanistic Education and Development, 34,* 171–181.

Sadker, D. M., Sadker, M. P., and Zittleman, K.R. 2008). *Teachers, schools, and society.* Boston, MA: McGraw Hill.

Samuels, S. J. (2002). Reading fluency: Its development and assessment. In A. Farstrup and S. J. Samuels (Eds.). *What research has to say about reading instruction,* 166–183. Newark, DE: International Reading Association

Santrock, J. W. (2004). *Educational psychology* (second ed.). New York: McGraw Hill.

Sheppard, L. (2001). The role of classroom assessment in teaching and learning. In V. Richardson's (Ed.). *Handbook of research on teaching (4th ed.).* Washington, DC: American Educational Research Association, 1066–1101.

Shi, B., Cao, X., Chen, Q., Zhuang, K., and Qui, J. (2017). Different brain structures associated with artistic and scientific creativity: a voxel-based morphometry study. Scientific Reports, 7. Rep. 7, doi: 10.1038/srep42911.

Stanovich, P. J. and Stanovich, K. E. (2003). *Using research and reason in education: How teachers can use scientifically based research to make curriculum and instructional decisions.* Jessup, MD: National Institute for Literacy.

Sternberg, R. (1996). *Successful intelligence: How practical and creative intelligence determine success in life.* New York: Plume

Sternberg, R. J. and Williams, W. M. (2010). *Educational psychology.* Boston, MA: Allyn and Bacon.

Strauss, S. L. (2011). Reading theory, constructivist psychology, and emerging concepts in neuroscience: Implications for a model of human consciousness. *Functional Neurology, Rehabilitation, and Ergonomics, 1(1),* 149–161.

Strauss, S. L. (2014). The political economy of dyslexia. *Monthly Review* 66(4), 35–47.

Stringfield, S. and Teddlie, C. (1991). Schools as affecters of teacher effects. In H. Waxman and H. Walberg (Eds.), *Effective teaching: Current research.* Berkeley, CA: McCutchan Publishing Corporation, 161–179.

Talbot, M. (1991). *The holographic universe.* New York. HarperPerennial.

Tart, C. (1996). Parapsychology and transpersonal psychology. In B. Scotton, A. Chinen, and J. Battista (Eds.). *Textbook of transpersonal psychiatry and psychology.* New York: Basic Books.

Vygotsky, L. S. (1978). *Mind in society: The development of higher psychological processes.* Cambridge, MA; Harvard University Press.

Von Bertalanffy, L. (1968). *General system theory: Foundations, development, applications.* New York: George Braziller

Walberg, J. J. (1991). Productive teaching and instruction: Assessing the knowledge base. In H. Waxman and H. Walberg (Eds.), *Effective teaching: Current research.* Berkeley, CA: McCutchan Publishing Corporation, 33–62.

Watson, J. B. and Rayner, R. (1920). Conditioned emotional reactions. *Journal of Experimental Psychology, 3,* 1–14.

Watson, J. B. and Rayner, R. (1920). Conditioned emotional reactions. *Journal of Experimental Psychology, 3,* 1–14.

Weaver, C. (2009). *Reading process*. Portsmouth, NH: Heinemann.

Woolfolk, A. (2007). *Educational psychology*. (10th ed.). Boston, MA: Pearson Educational, Inc.

Wurdinger, S. (2005). *Using experiential learning in the classroom: Practical ideas for all educators*. Lanham, MD: ScareCrow Education.

Zeichner, K. M. and Liston, D. P. (2014). *Reflective teaching: An introduction* (second ed). New York: Routledge.

Index

developmentally appropriate practice, 61
Dewey, John, 128
disciplined inquiry, 91
discovery learning, 89, 92–93
discussion, t-talk, 130

educational philosophy, 155–157
elaborative rehearsal, 69
emotional intelligence, 123–124
emotional states, 21
emotions, 16
emotions, negative, 43
equilibration, 58
experiential learning, 128
expository teaching, 98, 99–101
eye movement, 15

foveal, 15

generalization, 31
gestalt, 14

Hattie, John, 101–102
heuristic, 137
high-road transfer, 80
holism, 117
holistic education, essential characteristics,
   120–121
holistic learning theory, 117–122
holistic learning theory, applications,
   123–133
holistic learning theory, defining attributes,
   119–120
humanistic education, 105–107
humanistic educator, 111–112
humanistic learning theory, 105–109
humanistic learning theory, applications,
   111–115
humanistic learning theory, principles,
   107–109
hunter lesson plan, 138–139, 139

immediacy, 35
individuation, 118
inductive analysis, 91
information-processing model, 67–72
integrated studies, 132–133
interconnectedness, 118, 121

Jensen, Eric, 18–21
Jung, Carl, 118

knowledge and memory, 74
knowledge, conditional, 81
knowledge, content, 5
knowledge, declarative, 81
knowledge, importance of, 17
knowledge, learners and learning, 5
knowledge, pedagogical, 5
knowledge, pedagogical content, 5
knowledge, procedural, 81
knowledge, teacher, 18

law of effect, 34
law of exercise, 34
learning, 4, 17
learning, cognitive learning theory, 57
learning, cognitive perspective, 79–82
learning, constructivist view, 86–88
learning, importance of knowledge, 81–82
learning, laws of, 34, 45–46
learning, massed vs. distributed practice,
   81
lesson plan formats, basic, 140–141
lesson plan, schema-building, 140
lesson plan, skills, 65–66, 141
lesson plans, assessment, 143
lesson plans, behavioral objectives,
   141–143
lesson plans, Danielson Framework,
   147–148
lesson plans, reflection, 144
listening skills, 126, 127
long-term memory, 70
low of readiness, 34
low-road transfer, 79–80

maintenance rehearsal, 68
meaningful verbal learning, 97
memories, constructing, 73
memory, 15–16
memory, cognitive perspective, 73–78
memory, elaboration, 78
memory, episodic, 73
memory, executive control, 72
memory, explicit, 74
memory, imagery, 77
memory, implicit, 74

Made in United States
North Haven, CT
12 January 2025

64336100R00098